Michael Collins and The Treaty

His Differences with de Valera

T. RYLE DWYER

THE MERCIER PRESS
CORK and DUBLIN

The Mercier Press Limited
4 Bridge Street, Cork
24 Lower Abbey Street, Dublin 1

ISBN 0 85342 855 7

This edition 1988

To Honor O'Connor

Printed by Litho Press Co., Midleton, Co. Cork.

Contents

Preface

As an immigrant in his mid-twenties Michael Collins told his sister Hannie that he was leaving London to return to Ireland in order to join those who were preparing to stage a Rebellion. She tried to dissuade him. 'They'll let you down, Michael,' she warned him. 'They'll let you down.'

Years later when she returned to Ireland, she was convinced that her prediction had been fulfilled. Her brother's sacrifice seemed forgotten. His memory was villified by political opponents and his name was being omitted from schoolbooks. He was largely unknown to the young people of Ireland.

As the American-born son of American parents the name of Michael Collins meant nothing to me growing up in Ireland during the 1950s and early 1960s. Indeed I cannot remember his name being even mentioned in school. Had not a military barracks been named after him I would probably not have heard of him. My interest in this period of Irish history was only awakened while at university in the United States. Taking a course on European history between the two World Wars, I decided to write a term paper on the Treaty controversy which led to the Irish Civil War. Having assumed that the controversy surrounded the partition question, I was surprised to learn otherwise. I later expanded that study into a Master's thesis.

Since then I have retained a lively interest in the Treaty controversy, especially in the role played by Michael Collins, which I feel has not been adequately examined. Throughout history there are too many examples of leaders putting their own political and personal considerations before those of their fellow countrymen. Michael Collins has been accused of doing just that in signing the Anglo-Irish Treaty. Yet, in my opinion, it is a cruel irony that he should be so accused, seeing that he was the most reluctant of all the negotiators in London. He went there out of a sense of duty, with a keen appreciation of the likely outcome for his own popularity. When he eventually signed the Treaty, he did so with the prophetic awareness that he was signing his own death warrant.

While Eamon de Valera figures prominently throughout this study, it is primarily about Collins. In some instances, therefore, it has been necessary to summarise de Valera's views, but I have dealt with these summarised arguments in much greater detail in two books about de Valera which I have already written — one, a short biography in the Gill's Irish Lives series, has already been published, while the other is due to be published shortly after this work comes out.

I would like to thank the people who have helped me in numerous ways — among them those people who answered my letters while at university. These included Robert Barton, Ernest Blythe, Sir Geoffrey Shakespeare, Seán Mac Eoin, Liam Cosgrave, Lord Longford, Lord Birkenhead, Keith Middlemas, and Robert T. Reilly. I would like to acknowledge my debt to those who have facilitated me by allowing me to see documents in their possession, especially Liam Collins of Clonakilty for trusting me with the papers of his late uncle Michael Collins; John Pierse of Listowel for allowing me to hear family tapes; Nanette Barrett of Tralee for trusting me with papers of her late uncle Austin Stack; and David Adare Fitz-Gerald for furnishing me with a tape of his interview with Hannie Collins from which I have already quoted in this preface. I would also like to thank the various libraries that have facilitated me, especially the staff in the Kerry County

Library, in the Archives of University College, Dublin, in the Manuscript division of Trinity College, Dublin, in the National Library of Ireland, and in the State Paper Office, Dublin. Finally I would like to thank my mother and my brother, Seán, for their suggestions, and those other people who were so helpful in different ways, especially Michael Costello, Declan Keane, and Bob MacSweeney.

TRD

Tralee

1. Trouble between the Big Fellow and the Long Fellow

'That Long Whore won't get rid of me as easy as that,' Michael Collins was reported to have said after President Eamon de Valera tried to send him on a mission to the United States at the height of the Black and Tan war in January 1921.[1] This incident was one of the first signs of trouble between those giants of the Irish struggle for independence.

Collins had previously been an ardent admirer of de Valera, though neither could really have known the other very well, seeing that the former had only been a minor figure when the various separatist factions coalesced under the Sinn Féin banner in October 1917. He only rose to real prominence while de Valera and the other principal leaders of the movement were in jail for their supposed part in the so-called German Plot of May 1918.

As a member of the Supreme Council of the Irish Republican Brotherhood (IRB) and as Director of Organisation of the Irish Volunteers, Collins began to prepare for a renewal of the armed struggle against Britain. Desmond Ryan recalled an incident at Cullenswood House one day when Collins happened to pick up the old copy of *An Claidheamh Soluis* in which Patrick Pearse had announced the founding of the Irish Volunteers. Though Collins had many reservations about Pearse, he was enthusiastic about that piece of writing. 'We must accustom ourselves to the thought of arms, to the sight of arms, to the use of arms,' he read aloud with a blazing enthusiasm. 'We may make mistakes in the beginning and shoot the wrong people; but bloodshed is a cleansing and sanctifying thing, and the nation which regards it as that final horror has lost its manhood. There are things more horrible than bloodshed; and slavery is one of them.'[2] There was no doubt that those were sentiments with which Collins concurred — no matter what he personally thought of Pearse's leadership during the Easter Rebellion.

De Valera, who was considered a military genius by many within the movement, was the logical choice to lead a renewed struggle. He was not only the sole surviving commandant of the Rebellion but was also the officer whose men had inflicted by far the heaviest casualties on the British. Thus Collins went over to Britain in order to supervise efforts to help him to escape from Lincoln Gaol on 3 February 1919.

With the success of the escape, Collins obviously thought the time was right to renew the armed struggle. 'As for us on the outside,' he wrote to a jailed IRB colleague the following week, 'all ordinary peaceful means are ended and we shall be taking the only alternative actions in a short while now.'[3]

De Valera believed, however, that the movement's best chance of success would be by enlisting the support of international opinion. He therefore revealed that he planned to go to the United States in order to secure American help for the Irish cause. Efforts to dissuade him were unsuccessful.

'You know what it is like to argue with Dev,' Collins told a friend. 'He says he thought it out while in prison, and he feels that the one place where he can be useful to Ireland is in America.'[4]

While de Valera was in Britain awaiting a ship to the United States, the British released the other members of Sinn Féin who were being held in connection with the supposed German Plot, so he was free to return to Ireland with the others without being apprehended. He therefore went back in order to attend his first meeting of Dáil Éireann, the revolutionary assembly established in January 1919 by the representatives of Sinn Féin who had refused to take their seats at Westminster. The Dáil had plans to elect him *Priomh Aire* in succession to Cathal Brugha, who had been elected in his absence.

Preparations were made to stage a great public welcome. A letter was published in the press on behalf of Sinn Féin announcing that de Valera would be given a civic reception. He was to be met by the Lord Mayor and presented with the keys of the City of Dublin, an honour last bestowed on Queen Victoria. He prepared a defiant speech for the occasion, but it was never delivered, because British authorities banned the welcoming reception.

Sinn Féin was suddenly faced with a dilemma. Going ahead would undoubtedly provoke a confrontation, but some people argued that backing down would be fatal to the party's morale. They compared the occasion with the disastrous withdrawal at Clontarf during O'Connell's Repeal Movement. There was therefore some serious soul-searching when the Sinn Féin executive met in Dublin.

After one of the joint secretaries — under whose names the letter appeared in the press announcing the welcoming plans — revealed that he had nothing to do with issuing any such letter, Collins admitted that he had personally written it and signed the names himself. One of those present at the meeting recalled that Collins spoke 'with much vehemence and emphasis', making it clear that he was looking for a confrontation with the British. 'Ireland was likely to get more out of a general state of disorder than from a continuation of the situation as it then stood,' he declared according to Darrell Figgis. 'The proper people to take decisions of that kind were ready to face the British military, and were resolved to force the issue. And they were not to be deterred by weaklings and cowards.'[5]

On learning of the controversy, de Valera asked that the demonstations be cancelled rather than risk a confrontation in which lives might be lost. 'We who have waited,' he advised the party executive, 'know how to wait. Many a heavy fish is caught even with a fine line if the angler is patient.'[6] He was certain that matters of much greater principle would arise in which it would be better to take a defiant stand. His advice was heeded and the confrontation that Collins was looking for was thus postponed until after de Valera's departure for the United States in June 1919. It was not the last time that the two men would seem to be on opposite sides concerning the question of using a moderate approach.

In the following months Collins, who had been appointed Minister for Finance in de Valera's revolutionary government, was widely attributed with responsibility for the militant actions of the Irish Volunteers, which became known as the Irish Republican Army (IRA). Aided by a brilliant intelligence system organised by Collins, the IRA disrupted British rule in Ireland and gradually provoked a violent reaction in the form of the Black and Tan terror. While the Irish people may have disapproved of the activities of the IRA, they were utterly revolted by the reactions of the Black and Tans — all of which contributed largely to the 'general state of disorder' that Collins had advocated months earlier.

Meanwhile de Valera, who substituted the title of President for that of *Priomh Aire* because of its stronger appeal for Americans, toured the United States calling for American diplomatic recognition, gathering funds for the struggle at home, and generally trying to secure as much propaganda mileage as possible for the Irish cause. In the process he became involved in a bitter feud with some Irish-Americans, especially the leadership of the IRB's American affiliate, Clan na Gael, which was effectively controlled by Judge Daniel Cohalan of the New York Supreme Court and John Devoy, editor of the *Gaelic American*.

'I realised early,' de Valera wrote, that 'big as this country is it was not big enough to hold the judge and myself.' The dispute was really over who would act as American spokesman for the Irish cause. The Irish-Americans felt that de Valera should keep out of American politics and leave the field to them, while he was not about to let them determine political tactics 'without consultation and agreement' with himself. 'On the ways and means they must be consulted,' he wrote, 'but I reserve the right to use my judgement as to whether any means suggested is or is not in conformity with our purpose.'[7]

De Valera apparently convinced himself that it was for the good of the Irish cause that he should personally be seen to be in control of all tactics being used by the Irish-Americans, even when it came to the formulation of an Irish plank in the election platforms of the American political parties. For example, when Cohalan persuaded a committee of the Republican Party to include a plank recognising the right of the Irish people to self-determination, de Valera, who had failed in his own bid to get a plank accepted, undermined the Cohalan plank on the grounds that people might think the judge 'was the power behind our movement — the man to whom they would have to go. Were I to allow myself to appear thus as a puppet, apart from any personal pride, the movement would suffer a severe blow.'[8] In the light of subsequent events, it was significant that he actually mentioned his *personal pride* before referring to the interests of the movement.

Although the feud with Clan na Gael leaders was basically the result of a power struggle, it only surfaced publicly after de Valera had given a controversial interview to a correspondent of the *Westminster Gazette*. He had decided to give the interview in order to undermine a widespread American belief that Britain needed to hold on to Ireland for legitimate security reasons. As that belief was seriously hampering Irish efforts to enlist American sympathy, de Valera offered to satisfy Britain's legitimate security needs by either agreeing to the permanent neutralisation of Ireland, to a settlement on the lines of a 1901 treaty between the United States and Cuba (in accordance with which the latter guaranteed that her territory would never be used by an outside power), or by co-operating with the implementation of a kind of British Monroe Doctrine for the British Isles. When Cohalan and Devoy denounced those suggestions as a surrender offer to Britain, the resulting dispute was seen in the over-simplified terms of an ideological conflict between the anglophobia of the 'professional' Irish-Americans and the more moderate, progressive views of de Valera.

Even though the President issued a convincing clarification showing that he had not been offering to surrender, the *Gaelic American* remained so critical of the interview that it became necessary to send an emissary back to the Dáil to explain what was happening. Patrick McCartan, the emissary, told the cabinet that de Valera had simply been trying to get the British to start negotiating by showing 'that Ireland was willing to discuss safeguards for English security compatible with Ireland's independence.'[9]

Defence Minister Cathal Brugha 'showed marked hostility to the proposals' according to McCartan, but Arthur Griffith, the acting President, and Collins shut down the discussion and secured the cabinet's acceptance of the explanation. The President then went on to repeat throughout the United States the moderate views expressed in the *Westminster Gazette* interview, thereby securing for himself the distinct reputation of a moderate.

The British responded by sending out peace-feelers intimating that a settlement on the lines of Dominion Status, or Dominion Home Rule as it was called, might be possible. But suspecting that those overtures were only a smoke screen to obscure Britain's simultaneous efforts to suppress the IRA, Collins showed little enthusiasm, with the result that he got the reputation of being a hardliner.

In August 1920 Collins gave his first ever interview to the celebrated American correspondent, Carl W. Ackerman, whose previous journalistic scoops had included an interview with Lenin during the Russian Revolution. In the course of the interview, an account of which was published in the *Philadelphia Public Ledger*, Collins emphasised that there would 'be no compromise and no negotiations with any British Government until Ireland is recognised as an Independent Republic.'[10]

'But Mr Collins,' Ackerman asked, 'would you not consider accepting Dominion Home Rule as an installment?'

'I see you think we have only to whittle our demand down to Dominion Home Rule and we shall get it,' Collins replied. 'This talk about Dominion Home Rule is not prompted by England with a view to granting it to us, but merely with a view of getting rid of the Republican movement. England will give us neither as a gift. The same effort that would get us Dominion Home Rule will get us a Republic.'

John Devoy tried to use the hardline approach adopted in that interview to undermine de Valera's authority by depicting Collins as the real Irish leader in a *Gaelic American* editorial headed, 'Michael Collins Speaks for Ireland'. He followed that up in the next issue with a picture of Collins placed prominently on the front page under the caption, 'Ireland's Fighting Chief'.[11]

When the *Gaelic American* carried a report to the effect that there was a serious split within Sinn Féin in which Collins was at loggerheads with moderates like de Valera and Griffith, Collins denounced the report and eventually went so far as severing the IRB's ties with Clan na Gael over the latter's dispute with de Valera. 'Every member of the Irish cabinet is in full accord with President de Valera's policy,' Collins wrote to Devoy. 'When he speaks to America he speaks for us all.'[12]

Denouncing the rumours of a split between moderates and militants within Sinn Féin, Griffith publicly charged that the reports were inspired as part of a plot which had been hatched within Dublin Castle to assassinate prominent members of Sinn Féin. 'I am the first on the list,' he said. 'They intend to kill two birds with one stone by getting me and circulating the story I have been assassinated by extremists because I am a man of moderate action.'[13]

Through his intelligence network Collins learned of the existence of an undercover squad, known as the Cairo Gang, which had apparently been involved earlier in the year in the murder of the Lord Mayor of Cork, Thomas MacCurtain. His killers had made some crude efforts to make it appear that the assassination was part of an internal feud within Sinn Féin. Thus Collins was understandably suspicious of British peace feelers, especially during October and November 1920 when the British Prime Minister was publicly declaring that it would first be necessary to defeat the terrorists before peace would be possible, yet he was at the same time making peace overtures through two intermediaries, Patrick Moylett, a London-based Irish businessman, and John Steele, a correspondent of the *Chicago*

Tribune.

On 16 November Griffith gave Moylett a letter agreeing to 'a truce and a conference unhampered by preliminary conditions between representatives of the British Government and representatives of Dáil Éireann.'[14] On delivering the letter to Lloyd George personally, Moylett explained that he believed that Griffith would be prepared to accept a settlement subordinating Ireland's foreign affairs to Britain and proscribing an Irish Navy. The Prime Minister decided to take the weekend to think over his next move.

That was an eventful weekend in Ireland. After much careful consideration, some members of the Cairo Gang were marked for assassination, and men under the direction of Collins carried out some fourteen killings on Sunday morning. Of those, most were members of the gang, but some British soldiers also happened to get in the way.

'I found out that those fellows we put on the spot were going to put us on the spot,' Collins later told a British officer, 'so I got in first. Of course a few of your fellows, whom we didn't want to kill because we had nothing against them, walked on to the spot and had to be done in as they became dangerous evidence.'[15]

The furore over the killings was undoubtedly tempered by the actions of the Black and Tans who raided a football game at Croke Park that afternoon and began shooting indiscriminately into the crowd, killing fourteen people and wounding scores. Two of Collins' men, who were captured the previous night, were maltreated while in custody and then killed. Collins felt their loss so keenly that he personally helped dress their bodies in Volunteer uniforms and assisted in carrying the coffins. In fact, he took such a prominent part in the obsequies that he was filmed at the grave side.

He was taking a tremendous risk as Castle authorities

were undoubtedly keeping a close eye on the funeral. While most of them did not know what Collins looked like, he was well-known to many people in the crowd and there was a real danger that somebody might give him away inadvertently.

'Look!' said one woman at the cemetery, 'There's Mick Collins.'

Turning and glaring at her he snapped, 'You bloody bitch.'[16] He did not suffer fools gladly.

In the following days the demands for peace became even louder. Griffith explained to Steele that he would do all that he could to stop the violence, but the British would have to do what they could to call off the reprisals.

Lloyd George felt, however, or at least he pretended to believe that it would not be politically possible for him to engage in talks with either Collins or Brugha. He told AE (George Russell) that he was anxious to negotiate but could not talk with them. He also made it clear that recognising the Republic would be out of the question. 'We will not tolerate a Republic but anything short of that,' the Prime Minister said.[17]

The possibility of talks seemed to suffer a serious setback the same day in Dublin when Griffith was arrested and replaced by Collins as acting President. Nevertheless in the following days Lloyd George actually made his most serious bid to get talks going. On 1 December 1920 he persuaded Patrick J. Clune, the Roman Catholic Archbishop of Perth, Australia, to go to Ireland as an emissary to arrange a truce. The archbishop met with Griffith in Mountjoy Jail and was afterwards put in touch with Collins, who was of the opinion that the latest British overture was 'entirely dishonest.'[18] But, as Griffith thought otherwise, Collins got the cabinet's approval for a truce on condition that the acts of violence were suspended on both sides and that 'the entire Dáil' would be free to meet without interference with its peaceful activities.

A figurative spanner was thrown into the whole works, however, when Father Michael O'Flanagan, a Vice-President of Sinn Féin, appealed publicly to Lloyd George for a truce. Collins, immediately appreciating the significance of the unauthorised act, called on the party's acting secretary to disavow O'Flanagan's actions immediately. 'We must not,' he wrote, 'allow ourselves to be rushed by these foolish productions, or foolish people, who are tumbling over themselves to talk a "truce", when there is no truce.'[19] But the damage was already done. The British seemed to get the impression that the rebels were in trouble and were looking for a truce in order to avert imminent defeat, and this impression was deliberately fuelled by reports from Ireland contending that British forces were on the brink of victory.

On returning to London, Archbishop Clune found a distinct hardening in the attitude of the Prime Minister, who now insisted that he would not be able to negotiate with Collins or Richard Mulcahy, the IRA's chief of staff. He added that things would be simplified if they were to leave the country for a while. The archbishop had the impression that Lloyd George looked on Father O'Flanagan's appeal as 'showing of the white feather.'[20]

Lloyd George informed the House of Commons of the introduction of martial law in some southern counties and announced that after a specified date the death penalty would be enforced in the martial law area for the possession of arms or sheltering of rebels. He added that it would be possible to give 'safe conduct' to some members of the Dáil 'to meet to discuss peace proposals' but made it clear that there could be no such consideration for others.[21]

The archbishop returned to Dublin and told Griffith

what had transpired in London. On explaining that the British were now insisting that arms should be given up, Griffith replied that it amounted to a surrender, and he warned 'there would be no surrender, no matter what frightfulness was used.'[22]

Collins, who was in daily touch with Griffith, was obviously exasperated by the latest news. 'It seems to me,' he wrote to Griffith, 'that no additional good result can come from further continuing these discussions. You will understand that I am looking at it from an entirely utilitarian point of view. We have clearly demonstrated our willingness to have peace on honourable terms. Lloyd George insists upon capitulation. Between these there is no mean; and it is only a waste of time continuing.'[23] He was particularly disturbed that the British were exploiting the speculation about secret negotiations to mask their own militant activities, but he still agreed with a suggestion made by Griffith that the Irish terms for a truce should be re-stated.

Throughout, the archbishop's attitude was that Lloyd George wanted peace but was afraid of his own diehards, which Collins thought was being 'too credulous' of the Prime Minister's intentions. 'My own feeling about Lloyd George,' Collins wrote, 'is that we should not allow him to disassociate himself from his public actions, as head of his cabinet, and from the actions resulting from decisions of his cabinet. Particularly on this side, there is far too great a tendency to believe that Lloyd George is wishful for peace, and that it is only his own wild men prevent him from accomplishing his desires'[24]

Collins had a lengthy meeting with Clune on 18 December 1920. Afterwards he wrote that the archbishop and himself came to the conclusion 'that no more talk was necessary, seeing that the new proposal from the British Government was a proposal that we should surrender.'[25]

The British obviously thought that the Irish Republicans were on the point of cracking. The cabinet was told on Christmas Eve that arms were being surrendered in some quantities and 'stress was laid on the importance of doing nothing to check the surrender of arms at a time when the forces of the Crown had at last definitely established the upper hand.'[26]

Lloyd George was uneasy about agreeing to a truce when there were reports that his forces were on the brink of victory. Moreover, he was understandably reluctant to negotiate with a reputed radical like Collins, and word of the impending return of de Valera, a supposed moderate, gave hope that the moderates — with whom it would be easier to deal — might gain control of the movement. Instructions were therefore given that de Valera should not be arrested following his return to Ireland, but of course he was not aware of that fact, so he went into hiding.

One of de Valera's first acts upon his return was to suggest that Collins should go to the United States. In a long letter outlining the reasons for such a trip, the President stressed the economic, financial, strategic and propaganda benefits which could be gained, especially the opportunity it would afford Collins to secure valuable publicity for the Irish cause by demonstrating that he was 'moderate and full of common sense.'[27]

As was mentioned at the outset, Collins deeply resented the suggestion. So it was not long before there were signs of a power struggle between himself and the President on the lines of the one between the latter and the Irish-Americans. Yet there was very little ideological difference between de Valera and Collins. They were both moderate Republicans, desiring a conservative and rather romantic kind of Ireland.

'I stand for an Irish civilisation based on the people

and embodying and maintaining the things — their habits, ways of thought, customs — that make them different — the sort of life I was brought up in,' Collins explained. He went on to illustrate what he meant by recalling an incident which occurred during his immigrant days in London before the Easter Rebellion. 'Once, years ago,' he explained, 'a crowd of us were going along the Shepherd's Bush Road when out of a lane came a chap with a donkey — just the sort of donkey and just the sort of cart they have at home. He came out quite suddenly and abruptly and we all cheered him. Nobody who has not been an exile will understand me, but I stand for that.'[28]

According to Frank O'Connor's portrayal in *The Big Fellow,* Collins was a warm-hearted individual with a thoughtful and generous nature which was recognised by those closest to him. The first contact that many people actually had with him was when, as secretary of the National Aid Association, he enquired about their needs and provided them with money to get home following their release from prison. His concern for jailed comrades later led him to develop an extraordinary communications network with them, to work diligently for their escape, and to help plan some of their most successful escapes.

A sensitive person, Collins was easily moved to tears by the thought of poverty, loneliness, or infirmity, and was greatly troubled when his family and friends were victimised because of their associations with him. 'If I had recorded all the occasions when he wept,' Frank O'Connor wrote, 'I should have given the impression that he was quite hysterical. He wasn't; he laughed and wept like a child does (and indeed, as people in earlier centuries seemed to have done) quite without self-consciousness.'

While de Valera was in the United States, Collins

frequently visited his wife, bringing her money and news from America. She was thus able to keep her children together, unlike the period following the Easter Rebellion when she was left virtually distitute and was forced to move in with her parents and scatter her older children among relatives. Sinéad de Valera developed an affection for Collins, whose visits were undertaken at no small risk to himself. In later life she often spoke about how much the visits had meant to her at the time.

Although Collins had a charisma that inspired the intense loyalty of many colleagues, his rather contradictory personality also rubbed others the wrong way. He was a man of extremes who could switch from one extreme to another in a matter of moments. He could be quiet or boisterous, courteous or rude, open or secretive, thoughtful or inconsiderate, compassionate or ruthless, humble or egotistical, good-humoured or ill-tempered. As a result people who knew him well were sharply divided in their attitudes towards him.

Gerry Boland complained that he was a bully and a braggart, but Boland's brother, Harry, who worked closely with Collins within the IRB, felt differently.

'He's nothing of the kind,' Harry argued.

'You haven't seen as much of him as I have,' responded Gerry, who had been interned with Collins in Frongoch after the Easter Rebellion. 'In the camp, if he didn't win all the jumps, he'd break up the match.'[29]

Being highly competitive, Collins simply hated to lose at anything. When he had a good hand playing cards, for instance, he would be intense and would resent any interruptions, but when the cards were running against him, he would renege, look into his neighbour's hand, upset the deck and even jump on the likely winner and wrestle him to the floor. He was fond of wrestling, and it was not uncommon for him to come bursting into a friend's room looking for a 'piece of ear.' He would jump on the friend, and wrestle him to the ground biting his ear. Having forced someone into submission, he would give a crow of delight and look for someone stronger in a display of high-spirited exuberance that more than a few found rather irritating.

Desmond Ryan recalled that 'there were two Micks as you watched him in his small office, one, the jolly gasconading, hard-swearing good fellow; the other, a dour quiet man who lived with his life in his hand, heroic, dignified, a thinker, a fighter, a mystery.' If he talked to someone with 'humility, deference, and almost obsequiousness,' Ryan wrote, 'the one so honoured was surely an obscure figure in the world of Sinn Féin.' Though Collins was sometimes given to virulent outbursts, 'he was capable of the most generous and thorough-going apologies for his outbursts; saying with outstretched hand and a winning smile that he had been wrong and that he knew he was a hard man to work with.' Indeed he could be very difficult to work with, but Ryan explained that 'his scowl and his fist hammering on the table and his tornadoes of oaths and epithets were reserved for those of the highest rank in the movement. If you visited him in one of his offices and heard him addressing some visitor in terms of unmeasured fury with "these bloody fellows" and "lousers" singeing the air, and his watch flourished with fury in that visitor's face, it was a safe bet that the victim was a man very high in the Irish Republican Army who quite understood Mick's little way. If Collins was laughing and making withering personal remarks about his visitor's capacity or courage or efficiency, it was another safe bet that his visitor was at very least a cabinet minister in the Dáil.'[30]

Collins became particularly critical of Stack, the Minister for Home Affairs. 'Got plenty of staff, Austin?' he asked on entering Stack's office one day.

'Yes,' replied Stack.

'Well I have just received the following,' Collins snarled, throwing down a bundle of letters complaining about the Department for Home Affairs. 'Your department, Austin, is nothing but a bloody joke.'[31]

The rather sensitive Stack resented the remark. A few days later when someone referred to Collins as the Big Fellow, the nickname by which he had become affectionately known, Stack betrayed a knawing bitterness.

'Big Fella!' he said. 'He's no Big Fella to me.'[32]

Tom Barry, who was probably the most effective of the IRA field commanders, resented being called 'a windy west Cork beggar' by Collins for becoming a little unnerved after the two of them had been stopped in Dublin by the Black and Tans. At the time they were probably the two most wanted men in the country, so Barry's nervousness was understandable. Though irritated by the remark, he did not bear a grudge. Rather, he marvelled at the composure of Collins, who just talked his way out of such sticky situations.[33]

While the British believed that Collins travelled highly armed, well-protected, and elaborately disguised, he usually moved about Dublin alone, on a bicycle, unarmed and undisguised. Of course, the Black and Tans were at a disadvantage in looking for him when they had only one outdated picture of him, but he was known to detectives in the political division of the Dublin Metropolitan Police. Yet he had infiltrated them with his spy network, killed off their most efficient, and so terrorised the remainder that they were virtually impotent. They were apparently afraid to arrest him in public for fear that the faceless people who were believed to be protecting him would come to his rescue.

One can imagine the reactions of a detective on a Dublin tram when Collins sat down next to him and addressed him by name, enquired about the man's family and specific colleagues, cracked some jokes and, before alighting, assured the detective that he would be safe to get off, *when the tram reached its terminus*. As a result of such bravado, both real and imagined, Collins became a kind of folk-hero.

Ormonde Winter, who was in charge of intelligence at Dublin Castle, begrudgingly admitted to holding 'a certain respect' for his enemies among whom he singled out Collins as pre-eminent. 'Actuated by an intense patriotism,' Winter wrote, 'he combined the characteristics of a Robin Hood with those of an elusive Pimpernel. His many narrow escapes, when he managed to elude almost certain arrest, shrouded him in a cloak of historical romance.'[34] As a result he was credited with responsibility for exploits in which he had no involvement.

The ensuing notoriety was to cause some problems for Collins, especially with Brugha. Although the Defence Minister's reaction was widely attributed to jealousy, the charge was probably unfair because he was really a selfless character who never sought notoriety for himself. The problems between the two men were more likely the result of Brugha's dislike of the egotistical side of Collins' personality, coupled with resentment over the latter's interference in matters which were outside the scope of his official duties.

A man of enormous energy who prided himself in getting things done, Collins was not deterred by the nicety of minding his own business — a trait so graphically demonstrated when he took it upon himself to announce the welcoming preparations for de Valera's return to Dublin in March 1919. Collins also irritated people by being very curt when he thought they were wasting his time, which was understandable enough in the light of the tremendous amount of work he had undertaken.

Throughout the Black and Tan period, for example,

when he was the most wanted man in Ireland, Collins held down at least four major positions. He was Minister for Finance in the Dáil, Director of Organisation and Director of Intelligence in the IRA, and President of the IRB. In addition, he served as acting-President of the Dáil during December 1920. The voluminous correspondence that he engaged in testified to the energy he expended in each of those positions.

Faced with so much work, he tended to become irritable with those imposing needlessly upon his time. 'For God's sake,' he wrote to one officer in the habit of sending in pencilled reports which were difficult to read, 'buy a pen and a bottle of ink.' Returning another report that was written in an unintelligible hand, he commented: 'What in Heaven's name is the use of mystifying me with a thing like this?'[35]

One letter that Collins wrote to the cabinet secretary shortly after taking over as acting-President provides a rather typical example of the curt manner which antagonised many of his colleagues. 'Look here,' he wrote, 'I am not going to have any more of these parcels of miscellanies dumped on me. If anything concerns this department, or the general aspect, it should be sent to me and no more about it — I have something else to do than to wade through a miscellaneous collection of cuttings, surmounted by a letter from the Propaganda Department to you, a letter from you to the Propaganda Department, and another letter to myself.' He added that 'if a little commonsense is applied the situation will be very much simplified.'[36]

The chastened secretary immediately wrote to the Propaganda Minister suggesting that he write directly to Collins in future as 'it will save me a lot of trouble and abuse'.[37] In the face of Collins' withering criticism, some people did not want to work with him.

Collins himself apparently thought that the decision

to ask him to go to the United States was part of a scheme, inspired by critics like Brugha and Stack, to get rid of him. But Lloyd George's suggestion that he should leave Ireland for a while could well have been a factor, together with reasons given by the President in his letter suggesting the trip. There could be no doubt that de Valera wanted to get talks going as quickly as possible, and a visit to the United States by Collins would have the double advantage of putting further pressure to negotiate on Lloyd George while at the same time affording an opportunity of exploiting American opinion, which was one of Sinn Féin's strongest cards.

The President actually went so far as to suggest that the IRA's campaign should be waged so that it could be exploited for propaganda purposes in the United States. Although he had given up hope of securing diplomatic recognition, he was still mindful of the influential role that Americans could play in helping Ireland. He began adopting a policy which was strikingly similar to that being pursued by Lloyd George. On the one hand he tried to give the impression that he was a moderate who wanted to get talks going. In fact, he wrote a letter to the Prime Minister suggesting secret talks between them in January 1921. Yet at the same time he privately suggested changing the emphasis of the Irish campaign by scaling down the day-to-day military activities so that the IRA could concentrate on engaging the British in a major battle involving some five hundred men each month. In this way he felt that the Irish struggle would receive maximum publicity in the United States.

The British were already worried about the detrimental effect which their Irish policy was having on American opinion. At one cabinet meeting in December members of the British government expressed anxiety over the possibility 'of further compromising incidents which might even attain such gravity as to bring on us the intervention of the United States of America'. Lloyd George himself privately voiced disquiet a few weeks later over the effect that his government's policy was having on Anglo-American relations. 'In the interests of peace with America,' he told Bonar Law, the Conservative leader, 'I think we ought to see de Valera and try to get a settlement.'[38]

But Bonar Law, who was in the influential position of having a virtual veto over the coalition government's policy in view of his own party's majority in parliament, killed the possibility of negotiations at that point. He concluded that coercion was the only policy which was likely to be successful.

Responding to the intransigence of the British, de Valera tried to increase the international pressure on them by appearing moderate in his own public statements and interviews with the press. Rather than calling for recognition of the Irish Republic, he emphasised in some written answers to a French journalist that the Irish claim was simply for the right of self-determination, for which the Allies had supposedly been fighting during the First World War. 'If England should concede that right,' de Valera explained, 'there would be no further difficulties, either with her or with the Ulster minority. If Ulster should claim autonomy, we would be willing to grant it.' When asked if he would accept Dominion Home Rule, he intimated that such a settlement would be agreeable, seeing that even Bonar Law had publicly admitted that the Dominions had 'control of their whole destinies.' [39]

'Thus,' de Valera concluded, 'the British Dominions had conceded to them all the rights which the Irish Republicans demand. It is obvious that if these rights were not denied us, we would not be engaged in the present struggle.' He went on to stress that members of Sinn Féin were not radical isolationists. 'In fact,' he said, 'we are thoroughly sane and reasonable people, not a coterie of political doctrinaires, or even party politicians, Republican or other.' In subsequent interviews he proposed the establishment of an Irish confederation to settle the Ulster question, and he repeatedly emphasised his willingness to satisfy Britain's legitimate security needs.

The President flatly rejected advice that he take a firm stand by demanding recognition of the Irish Republic. 'In public statements,' he maintained, 'our policy should be not to make it easy for Lloyd George by proclaiming that nothing but so and so will satisfy us. Our position should be simply that we are insisting on only one right, and that is the right of the people of this country of determine for themselves how they should be governed. That sounds moderate, but includes everything.'[40]

The various moderate pronouncements were causing some concern within the IRA. Both Tom Barry and Ernie O'Malley, another of the army's more active commanders, recalled in their memoirs that they were troubled by de Valera's reputation as a moderate, but each was reassured on meeting him personally because he privately advocated engaging British forces in major confrontations each month.

To military people like Collins and Mulcahy, the proposal was absurd. The IRA simply did not have the numerical strength for such confrontations, but then de Valera obviously did not know much about the organisation's real strength. O'Malley was particularly surprised at how poorly informed the President was about the true military situation. On mentioning this to Collins and Mulcahy, the two of them were amused. In fact, they ridiculed some of the questions that de Valera had asked, much to the discomfort of O'Malley who later wrote that he 'resented their jokes at the expense of the

Long Fellow.'[41]

De Valera's own attitude towards Collins gradually became strained, as was evidenced by what, in effect, amounted to the latter's demotion from the position of deputy leader. The President designated Stack to take over in the event of anything happening to himself, even though it had been Collins who had taken over after Griffith's arrest. Just when the estrangement in de Valera's attitude actually developed is not known, but he told his authorised biographers that from April 1921 onwards 'Collins did not accept my view of things as he had done before and was inclined to give public expression to his own opinions even when they differed from mine.'[42]

Unlike the President who tended to portray a moderate public image while privately advocating a more hardline approach, Collins tended to do the opposite. Privately he was much more moderate than was generally believed, especially by the British. For example, Collins had been opposing some of the IRA'smore radical ideas, such as Brugha's efforts to have members of the British cabinet shot. At one point Brugha even suggested sending gunmen into the House of Commons. While de Valera was in the United States, Collins was appalled when Brugha proposed one such scheme to the cabinet.

'You'll get none of my men for that,' Collins declared.[43]

'That's all right, Mr Collins,' replied Brugha. 'I want none of *your* men. I'll get my own.'

Griffith, who was presiding at the meeting, was adamantly opposed to the idea. 'I shall never assent,' he emphasised. But Brugha was unmoved.

'Everybody knows where you stand, Mr Griffith. We have no illusions about you. We don't expect you to follow us. We don't want your assent for anything.'

Brugha later went ahead and called Seán Mac Eoin to Dublin and outlined for him a scheme to kill the whole British cabinet. Uneasy about the scheme, Mac Eoin complained to Collins, who denounced the idea as lunacy.

'This is madness,' Collins declared. 'Do you think that England has the makings of only one cabinet?' He suggested that Mac Eoin should talk to Mulcahy who ordered him to go home and forget about the project.[44]

This comparative moderation on the part of Collins also extended to his political views. In January 1921, for instance, he privately endorsed the development of the idea of Dominion Status for Ireland which, he admitted in a letter to Griffith, 'would be of advantage to us.'[45] Publicly, however, he continued to take the same kind of hardline stand which he had adopted the previous August. During a second interview with Carl Ackerman in April 1921, Collins indicated that the fight would continue 'until we win.'[46]

'What are your terms of settlement?' the reporter asked.

'Lloyd George has a chance of showing himself to be a great statesman by recognising the Irish Republic,' replied Collins.

'Do you mean a Republic within the British Commonwealth of Nations or outside?'

'No, I mean an Irish Republic.'

'Why are you so hopeful?'

'Because,' Collins explained, 'I know the strength of our forces and I know our position is infinitely stronger throughout the world. The terror the British wanted to instil in this country has completely broken down. It is only a question of time until we shall have them cleared out.'

'So you are still opposed to compromise?'

'When I saw you before I told you that the same effort

which would get us Dominion Home Rule would get us a Republic. I am still of that opinion, and we have never had so many peace moves as we have had since last autumn.'

The British actually concluded that there was a power struggle within Sinn Féin in which Collins was the real leader and de Valera was little more than a figurehead. They were certainly impressed by the apparent leadership of Collins as it gradually began to dawn on them that the predictions of the imminent collapse of the IRA had been overly optimistic.

'The tenacity of the IRA is extraordinary,' Tom Jones, a cabinet secretary, wrote to Bonar Law. 'Where was Michael Collins during the Great War? He would have been worth a dozen brass hats.'[47]

Faced with the realisation that victory was not at hand, Lloyd George again began thinking of negotiating a settlement. He thought that de Valera also wanted to negotiate but was being thwarted by the efforts of Collins trying to win a military victory.

'De Valera and Michael Collins have quarrelled,' Lloyd George told his cabinet on 27 April 1921. 'The latter will have a Republic and he carries a gun and he makes it impossible to negotiate. De Valera cannot come here and say he is willing to give up Irish Independence, for if he did, he might be shot.'[48]

The Prime Minister was anxious to negotiate but he was afraid of the political repercussions. If there was to be any chance of success, he felt that he would have to talk with Collins. The problem therefore was not so much whether he would negotiate, but whether it would be politically possible for him to meet Collins.

'The question is whether I can see Michael Collins,' Lloyd George told a confidant. 'No doubt he is the head and front of the movement. If I could see him, a settlement might be possible. The question is whether the

British people would be willing for us to negotiate with the head of a band of murderers.'[49]

The British cabinet discussed the possibility of arranging a truce in mid May 1921 in order to start negotiations. Lloyd George told his colleagues that while de Valera did 'not agree with the gun business,' he was in effect a prisoner of militants under Collins. Austen Chamberlain, who had recently taken over as Conservative leader noted that 'de Valera is at the mercy of Michael Collins.' And Lord Fitz-Alan, the Viceroy of Ireland, told the cabinet that 'you can't make a truce without meeting Michael Collins,' which he felt was out of the question at the time. 'We can't have that,' he concluded.[50]

2. Trapped for Bait

British efforts to depict themselves as coming to grips with Irish terrorism were made a mockery of on 25 May 1921 when the IRA seized and burned down the Customs House in Dublin. In the process the heaviest casualties since the Easter Rebellion of 1916 were inflicted, with the result that the incident received extensive coverage in the international press.

Initially the British decided to intensify their campaign in Ireland. Collins warned de Valera that he had learned that martial law 'of the most rigorous kind' was to be proclaimed throughout the Twenty-six Counties, where the British were going to treble their military strength and 'operate on a scheme of intense investment of areas, search and internment. All means of transport, from push bicycles up, will be commandeered, and allowed only on permit.'[1]

In order to implement these measures, however, the British needed popular support at home. They were afraid that there could be serious trouble if they further aroused public opinion, so it was decided not to enforce the new measures until after Sinn Féin had allowed the bill granting Home Rule to the Twenty-six Counties, which had been passed the previous December, to lapse on 12 July 1921.

De Valera kept his pressure on the British by reiterating his intimation that Dominion Status would be acceptable during an interview with a Swiss correspondent. 'The essential character of Dominion Home Rule,' he explained, 'is that Dominions are members of the British Empire, of their own free will. Most conservative statesmen like Bonar Law, have recognised the right of separation for the Dominions, if they find it to their advantage. It is evident that if England were to make such an offer, the *de facto* Republic would thereby be recognised.'[2]

Behind the scenes, however, de Valera was still anxious to maintain the Republican position, as he demonstrated when Collins got in touch with him about a priest who had written for permission to take the necessary oath in order to get a British passport to go to Australia. 'As an Irishman,' the priest wrote, 'I am not prepared to fulfil this condition unless such is in accordance with the wishes of the Irish Republican Government.'[3]

In the light of subsequent events it was significant that Collins was inclined to tell the priest to go ahead. 'I suppose,' he wrote to de Valera, 'there would be no objection to his taking the necessary oath or making the declaration as the case may be in the circumstances.' He nevertheless asked the President for guidelines in the matter.

'On account of the peculiar importance of the question of status for us just now, that is a question of recognition or non-recognition, we should seize the opportunity to fight it out if we can,' de Valera replied on 5 June 1921. 'The fact that the question arises in connection with the Church matter lends it additional importance. If we could create a sort of impassé by getting a number of young priests to refuse to take the oath, it would be excellent and most impressive as a protest.' In short, he was anxious to exploit the issue of the oath for propaganda purposes.

With the Irish determined to continue their campaign and the British prepared to intensify their efforts there seemed little prospect of peace. But then on 24 June 1921, the British altered their approach by inviting de Valera and 'anyone' he wished to accompany him to London for a conference to settle the Irish question. 'No

British Government in modern times,' Winston Churchill wrote, 'has ever appeared to make so sudden and complete a reversal of policy.'[4]

As Sir James Craig, the new Northern Ireland Prime Minister, had also been invited to partake in the proposed conference, de Valera did not actually accept the invitation. He was afraid that participating in such a conference would be tantamount to accepting partition before the talks had even begun. In addition, he told Jan Christiaan Smuts, the South African Prime Minister who visited Dublin incognito on 5 July 1921, he was afraid that Lloyd George would exploit the inevitable differences between the Irish factions and blame them for the possible failure of the talks. Before formally responding to the invitation de Valera explained that the British would have to agree to a truce.

Having played a major role in persuading the British to negotiate, the South African leader was anxious to be able to give the British cabinet some idea of the terms the Irish would be demanding. He therefore asked what kind of solution de Valera wanted.[5]

'A Republic,' replied the President.

'Do you really think the British people are ever likely to agree to such a Republic?'

In reply de Valera explained that the attainment of Republican status was so desirable that Irish representatives would agree to be bound by treaty limitations which would guarantee Britain's legitimate defensive needs, but he emphasised they would not be prepared to accept any restrictions under Dominion Status. The Irish people, he insisted, should have a free choice between a Republic with treaty limitations and the status of a Dominion without any limitations.

'We want a free choice,' the President stressed. 'Not a choice where the alternative is force. We must not be bullied into a decision.'

When Smuts argued that it would be a mistake to ask for a Republic, de Valera's response gave him grounds for hope.

'If the status of a Dominion is offered to me,' the President said, 'I will use all our machinery to get the Irish people to accept it.'

Back in London next day Smuts helped smooth the way with the British cabinet for a truce to come into effect on 11 July 1921. Once the terms had been agreed, de Valera consented to meet with Lloyd George in order to discuss how such a conference as that proposed could be set up.

On the evening the truce began, Collins called on de Valera and complained bitterly about being excluded from the delegation which was going to London. The President had chosen four members of the cabinet, Griffith, Stack, Plunkett and Barton, together with four others to accompany him, but he resolutely refused to include Collins, who made quite a scene over his exclusion. De Valera's authorised biographers contended that the President feared the negotiations 'might end in a stalemate and that war might be resumed, so he saw no reason why photographers should, at this stage, be given too many opportunities of taking pictures of Collins.'[6]

Next day the President and his entourage set out for London, where he intimated that Lloyd George and himself should meet alone. The Prime Minister jumped at the opportunity, and two of them had four separate meetings.

During the discussions de Valera's aim was to show as little of his hand as possible and try to elicit some firm British proposals. 'You will be glad to know that I am not dissatisfied with the general situation,' he wrote to Collins after the second meeting. Lloyd George had indicated that he was developing a formal offer. 'The proposal will be theirs,' the President added; 'we will be free to consider it without prejudice.'[7]

Before Lloyd George could present his proposals, however, there was a minor crisis when Craig, who was in London for separate talks, told the press that he was not concerned about de Valera's discussions, because those related to an 'area outside that of which I am Prime Minister.'

'Things may burst up here suddenly,' de Valera wrote to Collins, 'so all should be prepared.'[8] He was not about to let Craig's remarks go unchallenged for fear that this would be recognised as acceptance of partition. The President complained to Lloyd George that if the British supported Craig's remarks, then there would 'be no purpose in pursuing our conversations which would cease at once to be consistent with justice and honour and the interest of my country,'[9] He therefore asked whether the Prime Minister supported Craig's outlook, which the British leader neatly side-stepped by disclaiming any responsibility for Craig's remarks.

Next day the British presented formal proposals offering the Twenty-six Counties a form of Dominion Status, somewhat limited by defence restrictions, curtailing the size of the Irish army, prohibiting a navy, and insisting upon guarantees that Britain could obtain whatever facilities she might desire in time of crisis. The proposals, which included an insistence on free trade between Britain and Ireland, also stipulated that the new Irish state should 'allow for full recognition of the existing powers and privileges of the parliament of Northern Ireland, which cannot be abrogated except by their own consent.'

De Valera had actually anticipated proposals on those lines. 'I gathered,' he later wrote, 'that an offer of some form of Dominion Home Rule would be made, and I became convinced that if Ireland were willing to go within the Empire she could, by holding out, easily secure, *on paper at least,* the same nominal status and degree of liberty, that Canada and Australia enjoy, *except* as regards Ulster and naval defence. On both of these Lloyd George would be afraid to give way on account of the political opposition his doing so would arouse in England. With such an offer, and no alternative before them except that of continuing the war for the maintenance of the Republic, I felt certain that the majority of the people would be weaned from us.'[10] Thus even before he met Lloyd George to discuss the British offer, he was thinking of his own alternative proposals, which became known as External Association.

According to the British leader, de Valera indicated that he would accept 'the status of a Dominion *sans phrase*' on condition that consideration of the demanded defence concessions was deferred and all of Ulster became 'part of the Irish Dominion. Failing this,' he demanded, 'as the only alternative complete independence for Southern Ireland.'[11] The President promised a considered reply after he had consulted his Dáil colleagues, but made it clear that he was personally opposed to the British offer, which he found so unacceptable that he would not even bring the document back to Ireland himself. Instead he left it to the British to forward it by their own channels so that it could be considered in Dublin.

'There is, I fear,' Lloyd George concluded, 'little chance of his counter-proposals being satisfactory, but I am absolutely confident that we shall have public opinion overwhelmingly upon our side throughout the Empire and even in the United States when our proposals are published.'[12]

When the Dáil cabinet discussed the British offer upon de Valera's return, Brugha and Stack were unreservedly opposed, but the latter found that 'Griffith was favourable to the proposals save as to Ulster,' and he noted that Collins also seemed rather favourable, having 'described the offer as a great "step forward".'[13] Yet nobody suggested that the British proposals should actually be accepted.

The only advice that Collins had tendered to the President during the talks with Lloyd George was 'it would be worthwhile stipulating that, no matter how bad the terms are, they would be submitted to a full meeting' of the Dáil.[14] By so doing, the Irish could then insist on the release of all members of the Dáil being held by the British. Private representations were made for their release, and Dublin Castle announced on 6 August 1921 that all would be freed, with the exception of Seán Mac Eoin, who was under a sentence of death.

The refusal to free Mac Eoin prompted Collins to make another one of those unauthorised pronouncements which were so irritating to the President, who was actually trying to work for the release behind the scenes. He had already sent Barton to Dublin Castle to insist on Mac Eoin's release.[15] But suddenly the whole affair became a *cause celebré* when the *Irish Times* carried a statement issued by Collins to the effect that 'there can, and will be, no meeting of Dáil Éireann unless' Mac Eoin were released.[16] De Valera was therefore left with little alternative but to abandon his own low-keyed effort and declare publicly that he could not 'accept responsibility for proceeding further in the negotiations' if Mac Eoin was not freed.[17] The British cabinet then promptly reversed its earlier decision and released Mac Eoin.

After consultations with the cabinet de Valera formally rejected the British offer in a letter to Lloyd George on 10 August 1921. 'On the occasion of our last interview, I gave it as my judgement that Dáil Éireann could not and that the Irish people would not accept the proposals of your Government,' the President began. 'I now confirm that judgement.' It was significant, however, that the Dáil had not discussed these proposals and, indeed, did not even convene until six days later when it was asked to endorse the reply which had already been sent.

At the time the Dáil was composed largely of people selected by the leadership of Sinn Féin to represent the party. Since independent thinkers could be difficult to handle, individuals, who would give unquestioning support to the party leaders were usually selected. As a result all initiative in the Dáil was invariably left in the hands of the few recognised leaders. The general body of the assembly approved decisions rather blindly and took much for granted. As one member observed, 'nothing could well be less democratic in practice than the government which we recognised as the government of the Irish Republic.'[18]

Although Collins played little part in the contacts with the British during the following weeks, these must be considered in some detail, as must de Valera's overall attitude, because they were to have a profound significance afterwards. Both in the official reply to Lloyd George, which was largely drafted by Erskine Childers and approved by the cabinet, and in various contacts with people in touch with the British government, the Irish tactics were to appear willing to compromise on the question of Ireland's relationship with Britain on condition that partition was ended. In his formal reply, for instance, de Valera stated that 'a certain treaty of free association with the British Commonwealth group, as with a partial league of nations, we would be ready to recommend, and as a Government to negotiate and take responsibility for, had we an assurance that the entry of the nation as a whole into such an association would secure for it the allegiance of the present dissenting minority, to meet whose sentiments alone this step could be contemplated.' He added that the Ulster question should be something for the Irish people to settle themselves, but he agreed with the British demand that no force should be used to settle the problem.

'We do not contemplate the use of force,' he declared. 'If your Government stands aside, we can effect a complete reconciliation. We do agree with you "that no common action can be secured by force".'

In the light of previous events, this was a very significant declaration because a few years earlier de Valera had concluded that a British assurance that Ulster Unionists could not be coerced had undermined the Irish Convention,[19] when it was not prepared to accept partition. Now he was giving a similar assurance himself, so it was obvious that he realised that partition might have to be accepted as part of an Anglo-Irish settlement. In fact, he admitted as much during a secret session of the Dáil on 22 August 1921 when he said that if the British were prepared to recognise the Irish Republic, he 'would be in favour of giving each county power to vote itself out of the Republic if it so wished.'[20] The only alternative would be to use force, which he warned would be to make the same mistake with the North as Britain had made with rest of the island. If coercion was to be attempted, he said that the Unionists would get sympathy and support from all over the world.

Next day the President went so far as to admit that he was not excluding the possibility of any kind of settlement with Britain. He had previously indicated publicly that the support which Sinn Féin deputies had received at the polls had not been 'for a form of government so much, because we are not Republican doctrinaries, but it was for Irish freedom and Irish independence.'[21] Now, before allowing his name to go forward for re-election as President, he candidly told a private session of the Dáil that he did not consider that his Republican oath* bound him to any particular form of government.

'Remember I do not take, as far as I am concerned, oaths as regards forms of government,' he said. 'I regard myself here to maintain the independence of Ireland and to do the best for the Irish people.'[22] He was insistent that it would not prevent him from considering any proposals from the standpoint 'of what I consider the people of Ireland want and what I consider is best from their point of view.'[23]

'I cannot accept office,' he added, 'except on the understanding that no road is barred, [and] that we shall be free to consider every method.' The policy of the cabinet, he explained, would be to do what he thought best for the country and 'those who would disagree with me would resign.'[24]

He had already mentioned that he did not intend to be a member of any delegation which would go to London to negotiate a settlement. The question of who would actually go was debated at some length in cabinet. It had generally been felt that de Valera should head the delegation, but he declined for several reasons. He argued that whoever went would have to compromise and by staying at home he would be able to rally the Irish people to fight for an absolute claim rather than a compromise in case the fight had to be continued. He also

*The oath read: 'I. . . do solemnly swear (or affirm) that I do not and shall not yield a voluntary support to any pretended government, authority or power within Ireland hostile and inimical thereto; and I do further swear (or affirm) that, to the best of my knowledge and ability, I will support and defend the Irish Republic and the Government of the Irish Republic, which is Dáil Éireann, against all enemies, foreign and domestic; that I will bear true faith and allegiance to the same, and I take this obligation freely, without any mental reservations or purpose of evasion, so help me God.'

reasoned that as he was both head of state and head of the government, the delegates could always use the necessity to consult him as an excuse to prevent being forced to make hasty decisions. Moreover, he would be in a much better position to influence radical Republicans to accept a compromise agreement than if he were a party to the negotiations himself.

Neither Griffith nor Collins accepted the President's explanation. Along with Cosgrave, they insisted that he should go to London, but Brugha, Stack and Barton supported him. The President was thus able to use his own vote to exclude himself.

He then suggested that Griffith and Collins should lead the delegation. Stack entered what he himself described as 'a weak kind of objection' on the grounds that 'both gentlemen had been in favour of the July proposals.'[25] When Griffith objected to this assessment, Stack maintained that he got the impression that Griffith only wanted some modifications.

'Yes,' said Griffith, 'some modifications.'

Griffith was agreeable to act as chairman of the delegation but Collins was reluctant to serve on it at all. In arguing for his exclusion he made many of the same points that the President used in justifying his own exclusion. Collins pointed out that he would be better able to influence Republicans to accept a compromise settlement if he were not a member of the delegation. As the British considered him a treacherous gun-man, moreover, the delegation could always delay on the pretext of having to consult him, or demand further concessions in order to placate him. In that way the Irish representatives would be able to get the best possible terms from the British. In short, he was arguing that the British considered him the real leader, so the same arguments put forward by de Valera could also be applied in his own case.

'For three hours one night, after the decision had been made to send a delegation to London, I pleaded with de Valera to leave me at home and let some other man take my place as a negotiator,' recalled Collins, who even suggested that Stack should go.[26] But Stack flatly refused, as did Brugha.

'The point I tried to impress on de Valera was,' Collins added, 'that for several years (rightly or wrongly makes no difference) — the English had held me to be the one man most necessary to capture because they held me to be the one man responsible for the smashing of their Secret Service Organisation, and for their failure to terrorise the Irish people with their Black-and-Tans.' It really did not matter whether the legend was true, or was simply the product of press sensationalism, as Brugha believed. 'The important fact,' Collins emphasised, 'was that in England, as in Ireland, the Michael Collins legend existed. It pictured me as a mysterious active menace, elusive, unknown, unaccountable, and in this respect I was the only living Irishman of whom it could be said.'

'Bring me into the spotlight of a London conference,' he explained, 'and quickly will be discovered the common clay of which I am made. The glamour of the legendary figure will be gone for ever.'

De Valera was unmoved. 'His argument,' according to Collins, 'was that aside from whatever truth might be in my view the menace I constituted was of advantage to us.'

When the others refused to serve, Collins felt that he had no alternative but to go because 'it was a job that had to be done by somebody.' Over the years when something needed to be done, he had never shirked taking on the responsibility for doing it. Now was no different. 'I had no choice,' he explained afterwards. 'I had to go.'[27] But he made it clear to the cabinet that he was going against his better judgement. He was going, he said, as a soldier under orders.

After Griffith and Collins accepted the assignment, the cabinet sought three men 'to work in well' with them.[28] Only one of them, Barton, was a member of the new seven-man cabinet appointed following the President's re-election. Barton felt that he was appointed for propaganda purposes, seeing that he was a wealthy land owner and a member of what had been the Protestant ascendancy class. Two lawyers, Gavan Duffy and Eamon Duggan, were included as 'mere legal padding' in the President's words.[29]

In appointing Griffith and Collins, the President and the cabinet knew that they were appointing their most moderate members. The two of them were more favourably disposed to the July proposals than other ministers. 'That Griffith would accept the Crown under pressure I had no doubt,' de Valera admitted to a friend a few months later. 'From the preliminary work which M.C. [Michael Collins] was doing with the IRB, of which I had heard something, and from my own weighing up of him I felt certain that he too was contemplating accepting the Crown'. The President actually thought that he could use moderates like Griffith and Collins as 'better bait for Lloyd George — leading him on and on, further in our direction. I felt convinced on the other hand that as matters came to a close we would be able to hold them from this side from crossing the line.'[30]

De Valera had managed to secure the appointment of Erskine Childers as chief secretary to the delegation with a view to keeping an eye on Griffith and Collins to prevent them conceding too much. He believed that Childers, supported by his younger cousin Barton 'would be strong and stubborn enough as a retarding force to any precipitate giving away by the delegation.' With the two of them in touch with the cabinet in

Dublin, de Valera was confident that he would be able to hold Griffith and Collins from going too far.[31]

When the Dáil was asked to ratify the selection of the delegation Cosgrave moved that de Valers should head the delegation himself, but the suggestion was defeated on a division. On submitting the name of Collins for ratification, the latter explained that he believed de Valera should be part of the delegation so he 'would very much prefer not to be chosen.'[32]

'To me the task is a loathsome one,' he told the Dáil just as he earlier explained to the cabinet. 'If I go, I go in the spirit of a soldier who acts against his judgement at the orders of a superior officer.'[33]

If he was not a symbol of the Republic, the President explained he would go himself, but he felt that 'it was absolutely necessary that the Minister for Finance should be a member.' He added that Collins 'was absolutely vital to the delegation.'[34] With that, the nomination was promptly put to a vote and agreed.

The Dáil sanctioned the appointment of the delegates with full plenipotentiary powers. When one member tried to have their powers limited, de Valera — having twice previously threatened to resign if full plenipotentiary authority was denied to the delegation — objected. He said the Dáil would be able to reject the treaty after it was signed if it proved unsatisfactory.

'Remember what you are asking them to do,' the President said. 'You are asking them to secure by negotiations what we are totally unable to secure by force of arms.'[35] With that the motion was withdrawn.

The plenipotentiaries were afterwards furnished with credentials signed by the President authorising them 'to negotiate and conclude on behalf of Ireland, with the representatives of His Britannic Majesty, George V, a Treaty or Treaties of Settlement, Association and Accommodation between Ireland and the community of nations known as the British Commonwealth.' They were also issued with secret instructions, in accordance with which it was 'understood' that they would keep in touch with the cabinet on the progress of the negotiations, would furnish the cabinet with a copy of any draft treaty, and would await a reply before signing. Since the Dáil had already given the delegates full plenipotentiary powers to negotiate and sign a treaty as they saw fit, the cabinet's instructions — having been issued by an inferior body — were not legally binding in any instance in which they limited the powers of the delegation. But the plenipotentiaries did accept the instructions as a kind of informal understanding, so they were morally obliged to comply with them.

Meanwhile de Valera and Lloyd George had been exchanging letters and telegrams as they sought a basis on which to convene a conference. There were a couple of stumbling blocks.

Initially the President demanded that any talks would have to be based on Ireland's right to self-determination, while Lloyd George argued that the conference would only discuss the detailed application of Britain's July proposals. Even though de Valera modified his demand and requested that the conference should be unconditional, the Prime Minister tenaciously held his ground. In six of his seven communiques, he stressed that the conference could only discuss the July offer. In his last telegram on 29 September 1921, however, he surrendered on this point and suggested that the conference could 'explore every possibility' for a settlement 'with a view to ascertaining how the association of Ireland with the community of nations known as the British Empire may best be reconciled with Irish national aspirations.' This was actually a compromise by both sides on the positions originally assumed during the correspondence, but it appeared that de Valera had secured a tactical victory because he had taken the more flexible stand.

The second point at issue in the correspondence involved some diplomatic sparring. On first accepting an invitation to the conference on 9 September de Valera asserted that the Irish delegation would be representing a nation which recognised itself as independent. Collins realised at the time that the British would balk at this self-recognition. He warned Joe McGrath, one of the two couriers selected to bring the message to Britain, that the trip would be a waste of time.

'You might as well stay where you are,' Collins told him.[36]

Lloyd George promptly cancelled the conference when the text of the Irish message was released. Although de Valera later explained that he was only claiming self-recognition and did not expect the British to recognise Irish independence, the British were unwilling to have any confusion on this point. As far as Lloyd George was concerned there could be no question of Britain either recognising Irish independence or even accepting that the Irish recognised themselves as independent. He actually stressed that point on 29 September in his final telegram in which he renewed his invitation to the conference.

Thus, acceptance of the invitation involved yielding on the self-recognition issue, though de Valera's telegram, which was drafted for him by Griffith, did try to confuse the issue by stating that 'our respective positions have been stated and are understood.' This was an attempt to make it appear that the President was still insisting on the position taken earlier, but a close examination reveals the remarks did not constitute a condition, nor could they have been logically interpreted as an assertion that the British understood and accepted the Irish position because, of course, only the British could make such a statement on their own behalf. The statement was therefore an admission that the Irish understood and accepted Britain's insistence that there could be no conference if they persisted in claiming self-recognition.

'The communication of September 29th from Lloyd George made it clear that they were going into a conference not on the recognition of the Irish Republic,' Collins later told the Dáil, 'and I say if we all stood on the recognition of the Irish Republic as a prelude to any conference we could very easily have said so, and there would be no conference. What I want to make clear is that it was the acceptance of the invitation that formed the compromise. I was sent there to form that adaptation, to bear the brunt of it.'[37]

By making the July offer Lloyd George had strengthened his own hand immeasurably, seeing the proposals had been very well-received by the British press. Indeed, the only criticism had been that they were too generous, so he was in a position to enlist the popular support which his advisors deemed necessary to intensify their military measures to crush the IRA.

Collins was under no illusions about the need for compromise, if there was to be any chance of a settlement. In fact, he had already been publicly foreshadowing a willingness to compromise. In April he had explained in a letter to Carl Ackerman that he was standing for an Irish Republic without any qualification,[38] but on 26 August in some written answers to a United Press correspondent he defined that an Irish Republic 'means Irish freedom.'[39] The response seemed to be an indication that he was not unalterably attached to a republican form of government.

Little over a week later in Armagh, Collins revealed a certain amount of flexibility on the Ulster question when he told a public gathering that the Unionists of the Six Counties were being invited to join with the rest of the island. 'We can afford to give them even more than justice,' he said. 'We can afford to be generous. That is our message to the North.'[40] Yet in the last analysis, he knew that with the need to compromise it would not be possible to secure a settlement which would be acceptable to all at home.

'Of course, we all knew that whatever the outcome of the negotiations,' Collins wrote afterwards, 'we could never hope to bring back all that Ireland wanted and deserved to have, and we therefore knew that more or less opprobrium would be the best we could hope to win.'[41] This consideration was one of the main reasons for not wishing to be included in the delegation.

'I had got a certain name, whether I deserved it or not,' he later told the Dáil, 'and I knew when I was going over there that I was being placed in a position that I could not reconcile, and that could not in the public mind be reconciled with what they thought I stood for, no matter what we brought back.'[42]

'For my own part,' Collins explained on another occasion, 'I anticipated the loss of the position I held in the hearts of the Irish people as a result of my share in what was bound to be an unsatisfactory bargain. And to have and to hold the regard of one's fellow countrymen is surely a boon not to be lost, while there is a way to avoid it. But this consideration was not all what moved me to try to keep out of the negotiations.'[43]

There were at least two other considerations. One, he did genuinely believe that he could be of use to the delegation if he were 'kept in the background (against all eventualities) to be offered in a crisis as a final sacrifice with which to win our way to freedom.' Two, he was warned by a number of people that he was making a mistake in going to London while de Valera remained in

Dublin.

'I had warned Collins not to go unless de Valera also went,' Tim Healy wrote in his memoirs, 'but he was too unselfish and unsuspecting to refuse.'[44] Collins was unselfish in the matter, but he was not unsuspecting. He had misgivings about the President. Yet he still trusted him enough to suppress those misgivings. After all de Valera had candidly admitted not only that there would have to be compromise but also that some scapegoats were necessary. 'We must have scapegoats,' the President told a full meeting of his government.[45]

'Whether de Valera understood the advantage of keeping me in the background — whether he believed my presence in the delegation would be of greater value — or whether for motives best known to himself, he wished to include me among the scapegoats who must inevitably fail to win complete success is of little importance,' Collins contended. In the last analysis he had sufficient faith in the President to quell his own misgivings, though he was undoubtedly exaggerating when he later declared that 'before the negotiations began, no doubt of de Valera's sincerity had place in my mind.'[46] To his more intimate associates he admitted that he was being sent to do what his cabinet colleagues 'knew must be done but had not the moral courage to do themselves.'

'Let them make a scapegoat or anything they wish of me,' he told some IRB colleagues at the time. 'We have accepted the situation as it is, and someone must go.'[47]

'You know the way it is.' Collins wrote to his trusted aide Joe O'Reilly on the day the conference began. 'Either way it will be wrong. Wrong because of what has come to pass. You might say the trap is sprung.'[48]

3. Dublin — The Real Problem

When Collins appeared publicly in London on the eve of the conference, which began on 11 October 1921, he was in a buoyant mood. On the day before leaving Dublin he had become engaged to be married, and he gave the appearance of possessing all the confidence of youth. Still only thirty years old, he showed no outward sign of being overawed by the daunting task in front of him. 'He gave me the impression of a young colt set free in a field of lush grass.' one of the typists with the delegation later remembered.[1]

The task confronting the relatively inexperienced Irish negotiators was indeed a formidable one, especially for Collins. He was easily the youngest of the plenipotentiaries on either side, as all the others were in their forties or fifties. Nevertheless he was soon to find himself in the unenviable position of sharing much of the leadership responsibility over a bitterly divided delegation which obviously lacked the real confidence of the cabinet members at home. Yet he had to face a determined British delegation consisting of an experienced and seasoned team of politicians, headed by Lloyd George with the aid of the most powerful men in his government.

Notwithstanding his carefree appearance, Collins was troubled and uneasy within himself. He realised the enormity of the task confronting him and the dangers involved. Before leaving Dublin, people had given him all kinds of warnings about both his colleagues at home and the British. A priest friend had advised him, for instance, to go to daily mass and to shun all British hospitality by keeping strictly to himself while not in conference.

'I know fully the English method in these matters,' Collins assured the priest, adding that he was attending to part of the advice 'though not — for certain reasons — quite fully.'[2] He was not the inexperienced country boy visiting London for the first time as the priest might have supposed. Collins knew London well. In fact, he had lived there for over ten of the sixteen years since finishing school, with the result that he had numerous friends from his emigrant days to call upon.

Throughout the negotiations the Irish delegation refused British hospitality, but as the Irish party — which included advisers, secretaries, couriers, typists, and even a small domestic staff — was over thirty strong, there were ample opportunities for socialising among themselves. The party was housed in two separate buildings at 22 Han's Place and nearby at 15 Cadogen Gardens, where the delegation had its offices. Collins and the younger men stayed at Cadogen Gardens, while the women and older men resided at Han's Place.

Although Collins sometimes engaged in good natured horse-play with his friends, the late sleepers among whom he often awakened with a jug of cold water, he was never truly at ease during the negotiations. Like many other members of Sinn Féin he had the reputation of being somewhat anti-clerical, seeing that he tended to blame the conservatism of the Roman Catholic hierarchy for retarding the nationalist cause in Ireland. On at least one occasion, he actually called for the *extermination* of the hierarchy.[3] So it was probably indicative of the weight upon his mind that each day during the conference he used to slip out to early morning mass at a nearby church.

Collins immediately realised that he was ill-suited to diplomatic talks. He had little time for the endless beating around the bush on which such negotiations seemed to thrive. 'I have come to call a spade a spade,' he wrote on the opening day. 'It is the only name I know it by.'[4] But, of course, he soon found that he could not be as candid as he would have liked, with the result that the first day with its two plenary sessions was a particularly trying one for him. 'I never felt so relieved at the end of any day,' he wrote to de Valera, 'and I need hardly say I am not looking forward with any pleasure to resumptions — such a crowd I never met.'[5]

The British representatives did not even seem to trust one another, and Collins certainly had little regard for any of them, with the exception of Lord Birkenhead, whom he came to characterise as 'a good man'.[6] The Lord Chancellor had the reputation of being a hardened Unionist, but Collins liked him because he was clear and concise and was prepared to deal in practicalities. All the others he disliked with a varying intensity. Of course all of them were professional politicians and most were lawyers — two types of people for whom Collins generally had an aversion. He was convinced that the genial Lloyd George — whom he found 'particularly obnoxious' — and the latter's bombastic erstwhile Liberal colleague, Winston S. Churchill, were both unprincipled individuals who would do anything for political gain.[7] 'Churchill was as rude as could be,' according to Barton, who noted that the future British leader sat through the conference making paper boats and looking quite hostile. 'He always looked at us as if he would be glad to cut our throats, a very different attitude from Lloyd George, who was so affable.'[8] Austen Chamberlain, the Conservative leader, was more formal and reserved, but Collins disliked him because he not only found him too cold but also suspected that he was a snob who looked down on the Irish leadership. For Sir Hamar Greenwood, the Chief Secretary for Ireland and the most vocal defender of the Black and Tans, Collins had only contempt. He also disliked the Attorney General, Sir

Gordon Hewart, but he apparently left no account of his attitude towards the only other member of the British delegation, Sir Laming Worthington-Evans, the Secretary of State for War.[9]

From the outset the British took the offensive by insisting that their July proposals would have to form the basis of any agreement. The Irish representatives, on the other hand, were supposed to seek External Association, even though they only had 'a hazy conception of what it would be in its final form,' according to Barton. 'What was clear was that it meant that no vestige of British authority would remain in Ireland. The compromise would be as regards our foreign relations.'[10]

The delegation brought with it a partially completed document, known as Draft Treaty A, in which External Association was outlined in treaty form. But it was not really supposed to be the draft for a treaty, as has been suggested. Rather, it was a document designed for diplomatic manoeuvring.

De Valera had proposed that a series of draft treaties should be drawn up. Draft Treaty A, was simply supposed to be the outline of counter proposals which the Irish side would initially put forward for negotiating purposes. Draft Treaty B, on the other hand, was a propaganda document which would be published as representing terms that would be acceptable to the Irish side in the event that the negotiations broke down. De Valera gave Childers and Duffy incomplete copies of those two documents on the eve of their departure for London, but he did not attempt to draw up the draft of the document that the delegation should use for a contemplated treaty. The President explained that the plenipotentiaries would have to be responsible for that drafting. 'We must depend on your side for the initiative after this.' he wrote to Griffith.[11]

The essentials of External Association were that the British would renounce all rights to interfere in the internal affairs of Ireland and would acknowledge the country's complete independence in her own domestic affairs. At the same time Ireland would agree to be an equal partner with the countries of the British Commonwealth in a kind of partial league of nations.

Instead of the 'common citizenship' shared by citizens of the Dominions, who were British subjects owing nominal allegiance to the British King, External Association envisioned 'reciprocal citizenship' — the subtle difference being that the Irish people would be Irish citizens, rather than British subjects. Yet Irish citizens would have the same rights as British subjects while resident in the dominions, and British subjects would have reciprocal rights while residing in Ireland.

The distinction between reciprocal and common citizenship represented at the personal level the difference between External Association and Dominion Status at the national level. In each case there would be little practical difference but a significant symbolic distinction. De Valera himself later explained that External Association was designed to ensure that Ireland would legally have 'a guarantee of the same constitutional rights that Canada and Australia claimed.'[12]

Realising that the major problem would be Britain's attachment to her monarchy and its symbolic pre-eminence in the Dominions, the Irish delegates tried 'to hold back on the question of the Crown,' according to Griffith, 'until we knew what we were going to get in exchange for some accommodation regarding it.'[13] They therefore initially tried to concentrate on other issues like defence, finance, and partition. The conference decided to set up committees to deal with the more technical aspects of defence and finance. Collins was the only Irish plenipotentiary on those two Irish committees on which he was helped by some of his own men like Emmet Dalton, J. J. O'Connell, Eoin O'Duffy, and Diarmuid O'Hegarty, together with Erskine Childers, who quickly proved to be a particularly unhappy choice, as he was 'altogether too radical and impractical' in the estimation of Collins.[14]

Childers was not in the least reticent about pushing his own strong views. On the third day of the conference, he was with Collins when they met Churchill and the First Sea Lord, Admiral David Beatty, who was about to leave for Washington where he was due to represent Britain at the Naval Conference. 'Now, gentlemen,' Childers began, 'I mean to demonstrate that Ireland is not only no source of danger to England, but from the military standpoint, is virtually useless.'[15]

'This announcement staggered me probably more than it did the other two,' Collins recalled. 'It was ridiculous balderdash, I felt like wanting to get out of the room, but I naturally realised that I must make a pretence of standing by my colleague. Churchill and Beatty exchanged glances, and then gave Childers their attention again.'

'Take the matter of Irish bases for English submarine chasers,' Childers continued. 'From the viewpoint of naval expediency Plymouth is a far better base than any port on the Irish coast.'

'You really think so?' asked Beatty.

Childers insisted that such was the case. 'For instance,' he added, 'supposing Ireland were not there at all?'

'Ah,' said Beatty with a smile, 'but Ireland *is* there.'

'And how many times,' interjected Churchill, 'have we wished she were not!'

While the kind of hypothetical approach adopted by Childers would likely have been appreciated by the more theoretical mind of a mathematician like de

Valera, it had no appeal for the practically-minded Collins. The latter never even bothered to relate the details of the hypothetical argument, which he felt the British destroyed.

Using a map marking the locations of ships sunk by U-boats during the Great War, Beatty demonstrated that certain Irish ports were in some circumstances clearly more strategic than Plymouth for anti-submarine warfare. Childers had no real answer, much to the chagrin of Collins, who noted that he 'never felt more a fool' in his whole life.

'I had an idea,' Collins continued. Pointing to the French coast he suggested that Le Harve would make 'an excellent base for British forces engaged in hunting submarines.'

'Quite so,' replied the admiral with a smile, 'but we can't take a French port!'

'If that constitutes duress,' Collins later explained, 'I'll admit that we were under duress. But to my way of thinking it is plain talk, right talk, and the kind of talk I prefer my opponents to use.' Shortly after the meeting Collins wrote to his fiancée that he preferred people to be open. 'I like people to say what they themselves think and mean,' he wrote.[16] Yet even at that early stage of the conference he had found himself having to support arguments in which he did not really believe.

This happened again on 18 October 1921 after Childers submitted a memorandum to the British insisting on Ireland's right to defend herself. He was claiming, in essence, that the denial of this right was a denial of Ireland's 'existence as a nation'. But he conceded in the memorandum that 'Ireland would be very unlikely to plan the building of submarines which are eminently an offensive weapon out of harmony with her purely defensive policy.'

That concession undermined the Irish case, as far as

Collins was concerned. He felt the right to have a navy to defend the island was useless if Ireland were not to be allowed to have submarines, seeing that the Irish people simply could not afford to build a regular navy. Believing that attack was the best method of defence, Collins thought that submarines, which were comparatively cheap to build and easy to man, were the country's only hope of defending herself properly. So in renouncing the right to have submarines Childers had, in effect, undermined the Irish case by conceding 'a point that really mattered,' according to Collins, who declared, 'this cannot be stated too emphatically.'[17]

Of course Collins obviously realised that the defence concessions would have to be made, or he would not have allowed the memorandum to be given to the British in the first place. The difference between himself and Childers was that once he himself recognised the necessity to concede a point, he was prepared to carry the concession to its logical or practical conclusion. Yet, like one of those politicans he so despised, he still went through the motions of arguing the case for the country's right to defend herself.

'As a practical man,' he asked Churchill, 'do you think that we are going to build a big navy?'[18]

'Honestly,' replied Churchill, 'I do not, and why then should we get into these depths? Why should these questions be raised?'

'It is *we* really who are dealing with this in a practical manner,' Collins explained. But he did not personally believe in what he was arguing. He was therefore deeply uneasy within himself.

'Trouble everywhere,' he wrote to his fiancée next day. 'Last night I escaped all my own people and went for a drive alone.'[19] He admitted to feeling quite lonely and made arrangements for her to spend some time in London with him.

Collins was finding the negotiations especially trying in that he obviously felt he had to act as a politician himself. 'To be a politician,' he wrote to a friend, 'one needs to have the ability to say one thing and mean another; one needs to be abnormally successful at the "art" of twisting the truth. Can you wonder that I think and think yet never manage to achieve peace of mind?' He was afraid that anything he might say would likely be twisted and used against him. 'I do not in the least care for the false atmosphere of these discussions,' he concluded.[20]

In this frame of mind he tended to become somewhat undiplomatically irritable. During one committee meeting, Emmet Dalton recalled that Churchill was arguing some case with elaborately prepared points to which none of the Irish side was replying. 'Have we any answer to these?' Collins asked in a note scribbled to Dalton.

'No,' replied the aide.

Collins then listened for a while longer before suddenly becoming exasperated and slamming his fist on the table. 'For Christ sake,' he said, 'come to the point.'[21]

The loquacious Churchill was momentarily speechless. He sat there with a stunned expression upon his face. At that point Collins errupted with an infectious laugh which Churchill, in spite of himself, soon joined, thereby dissipating much of the force from his carefully prepared case.

But that was only a moment of light relief for Collins who was otherwise deeply agitated. The British were far from presenting him with his only problems. He not only found it necessary to hide his feelings from them but also from his own colleagues like Childers, who was keeping in touch with Dublin, where Brugha and Stack were likely to be prejudiced against anything acceptable to Collins himself. Indeed, it would not be long before

Collins would come to the conclusion that Dublin, not the British, was his 'real problem' in the search for a settlement.[22]

There was no Ulster clause in Draft Treaty A, for example, and the Irish delegation had to deal with the question at the third plenary session of the conference before the clause had arrived. Almost at once it became apparent that the Irish negotiating position had been weakened by de Valera's assurance that force would not be used to settle partition. 'We promise you,' Lloyd George said, recalling the President's assurance, 'to stand aside, and any efforts to induce [the Six Counties] to unite with the rest of Ireland will have our benevolent neutrality.'[23]

'It is not intended to use force, not because Ulster would not be defeated in a fight,' Collins explained, 'but because defeat would not settle the matter.'[24] He made it clear, however, that some provisions would have to be made for many of the nationalists who had been included in Northern Ireland against their will. 'If we are not going to coerce the North East corner, the North East corner must not be allowed to coerce,' he emphasised.[25] 'There might,' he added, 'be a plan for a boundary commission or for local option, or whatever you may call it.'[26] A few days later he went on to predict that there would be civil war if the Six County area were retained. Sinn Féin was prepared to meet with the Unionists and be reasonable with them, he maintained, 'but if they refused our proposals and declared they were going to hold our people under their control, then freedom of choice must be secured in order to enable the people to say whether they would come with us or remain under the Northern Parliament.'[27]

The Prime Minister asked what would be done about isolated nationalist areas within a Unionist stronghold, such as West Belfast.

'It would be necessary to make a deal,' explained Griffith.

Very well, Lloyd George replied, the Irish could deal among themselves. But Griffith insisted that the British would have to arrange the deal as they had created the problem in the first place.

The financial issue — the settlement of which was eventually entrusted to separate negotiations — never really posed a serious problem during the London Conference. When the finance committee met for the first and only time on 19 October 1921, Collins found that his advisers were really out of their depth against the British experts, but he fared well enough himself by taking the offensive.

The British were claiming that Ireland should undertake to pay part of Britain's war debt and such things as the pensions of those who had worked within the civil service in Ireland, but Collins countered that Ireland had been grossly over-taxed during the nineteenth century. So he argued that Ireland should start out afresh with a clean slate. 'If we go into all past details,' he said, 'you will find that you owe us money. I say let us get rid of all these details, and let us treat the past as the past.'[28]

With the British unwilling to accept that argument, Collins persisted. 'I will put some arguments that may surprise you,' he said.

'Mr Collins will never surprise me again', replied Worthington-Evans.

'According to my figures,' Collins declared, 'our counter-claim works out at £3,940,000,000.'

The British were staggered. 'I suppose that dates from the time of Brian Boru,' exclaimed the Chancellor of the Exchequer. 'How much did we owe you then?'

'Oh no,' replied Collins, 'it is the capital sum since the Act of Union. Of course I have included in my calculations your restrictions on our capital development.'

Finding himself poorly prepared and his advisers out of their depth, Collins secretly enlisted the valuable services of Joseph Brennan, who had been serving with the British administration in Ireland.[29] Even though Brennan was technically on the British side, Collins was always prepared to enlist the help of such Irish people, regardless of their past political affiliation. Some such people had indeed formed the backbone of his intelligence system. 'Never mind what the record of these people was in the past,' he advised Childers, 'let us assume now that they are in the Irish cause up to their necks.'[30]

Collins' choice of advisers was, nevertheless, causing problems with Dublin. De Valera wrote that Brugha felt he was in charge of the experts advising on defence matters and that consequently those advisers 'should have been summoned through him' so he 'would like to know *why* that course was not followed.' Likewise, the President added, the constitutional advisers should be summoned through Stack.[31]

Griffith responded accepting the principle, but by then nearly all of the advisers had already been chosen, so it did not matter. Yet it was another instance in which the delegation did not challenge an apparent infringement of its powers. The plenipotentiaries had been appointed by the Dáil and were answerable only to it, not to the respective members of the cabinet.

If Collins saw ominous implications in the President's letter, these were only minor to the sense of foreboding prompted next day when the delegation learned from the morning press that de Valera had sent an open telegram to Pope Benedict XV in response to an exchange of messages between the Pope and King George V.

The President had complained that in responding to a message from the Pope, the British King had expressed the hope that the negotiations would 'achieve a permanent settlement of the trouble in Ireland and may initiate a new era of peace and happiness for my people.' This implied, according to de Valera, that the Irish people owed allegiance to the King, whereas, he explained, Ireland had already declared her independence.

Although de Valera's inference was not unreasonable, the King's message was really vague enough to be interpreted differently. The whole matter was ambigious, as the President himself admitted in his own telegram to the Vatican. He had actually used the King's message as an excuse to take an indirect swipe at the Pope, whose telegram was the really irritating one from the Irish standpoint. 'By this message,' de Valera explained to Griffith, 'the Vatican recognised the struggle between Ireland and England as a purely domestic one, for King George, and by implication pronounced judgement against us.'[32]

Under the circumstances, therefore, it was understandable that Griffith and Collins were annoyed that while they were involved in tense and delicate negotiations, the President had — without even warning them — revived the self-recognition issue by insulting the British King in an attempt to chide the Pope. The affair also had a deeper significance in that it fuelled Collins' uneasiness. It seemed to confirm his suspicions that de Valera was preparing the ground to lay all the blame for any compromises on the delegation by covering up the fact that he had already compromised on the self-recognition issue by agreeing to the conference. Moreover, the publication of the telegram brought the allegiance question to the foreground of the negotiations, much to the chagrin of Griffith and Collins, who nevertheless managed to stall the British a little longer by agreeing to present the Irish delegation's first formal proposals the following week.

Before actually tackling the issue they tried to involve de Valera. Childers was instructed to write to Dublin for advice on the best way of approaching the allegiance problem. He explained to the President that the plenipotentiaries felt they could respond with an outright refusal to consider allegiance, or they could 'obtain a field of manoeuvre and delay the crucial question' by stating that if agreement were reached on all other issues, 'they would be prepared to consider the question of the Crown.'[33] Unfortunately the cabinet did not reply.

That weekend Collins returned to Dublin and pleaded with the President to go back to London with him, but de Valera refused on the grounds that there was no necessity at this juncture. He added, however, that he would go later if it could be shown that his presence was really required.

In an undated letter written to a friend during the negotiations, Collins alluded to his growing distrust of de Valera. 'I was warned more times than I can recall about the ONE,' he wrote. 'And when I was caught for this delegation my immediate thought was of how easily I walked into the preparations. But having walked in I had to stay.'[34]

The uneasiness which Collins felt about his cabinet colleagues at home was not alleviated by the reports that Childers was sending to Dublin. These included his own observations even when they differed from those of Collins,[35] who described the reports as 'masterpieces of half-statement, painting a picture far from the true state of things.'[36] He surmised as well — correctly as it turned out — that Childers was also sending secret reports to de Valera.[37]

This was an intolerable situation. Griffith had personally detested Childers for a long time, and now Collins and himself had come to look on the secretary as a kind of spy on the delegation. They therefore decided to eliminate him from the actual discussions by secretly suggesting to the British that Lloyd George should invite the two of them to a private discussion after one of the plenary sessions of the conference.[38]

Welcoming the opportunity of eliminating Childers, whom he believed to be undermining British efforts to win over Griffith and Collins, Lloyd George invited the two Irish leaders to meet Chamberlain and himself after the seventh plenary of the conference on 24 October 1921. Unaware that Griffith and Collins had actually requested the meeting, the other members of the Irish delegation did not realise that their own colleagues had inspired the abandonment of the plenary sessions, which gave way to twenty-four informal sub-conference meetings at which there were no secretaries. As a result Childers was excluded from the talks completely, while Barton was only invited to four of the sub-conference meetings — three of which were in the final thirty-six hours leading up to the actual signing of the Treaty.

It was later contended that at the last plenary session the Irish delegation gave in on the defence question. Lord Birkenhead had reputedly undermined the Irish argument by contending that if the Irish afforded Britain the defence facilities which British naval experts considered necessary, then no enemy of Britain would recognise Irish neutrality, with the result that the right to remain neutral being claimed by the Irish would be 'reduced to a shadow — a meaningless trophy which would give you nothing.'

'We accept the principle that your security should be looked after,' Griffith replied, 'though the working out of the details might be very difficult.'

With that assurance, Frank Pakenham (now Lord Longford) declared in his book, *Peace by Ordeal* that 'Britain had won on defence.'[39] But this ignored the fact that de Valera had long ago accepted the principle that Ireland would accommodate Britain's legitimate defensive needs. That principle had been at the very heart of his controversial *Westminster Gazette* interview and many of his subsequent statements. So Griffith's acceptance of the principle was in harmony with the views expressed by de Valera, who raised no objection to the concession.

But the President did take exception to some remarks made by the chairman of the delegation during the first sub-conference meeting. With the British insisting that Ireland would have to agree to the link with the Crown, Griffith reported that he explained 'if we came to an agreement on all other points I could recommend some form of association with the Crown.'[40]

Even though no mention was made of what form the connection with the Crown would take, de Valera assumed that Griffith had been thinking of allegiance. So when the Dublin-based members of the cabinet met to consider the report, the President asked whether those present would be willing to give allegiance to the British Crown. All answered in the negative, including Kevin O'Higgins. De Valera therefore wrote to the delegation that the possibility of agreeing to allegiance was out of the question:

> We're all here at one that there can be no question of our asking the Irish people to enter into an arrangement which would make them subject to the Crown, or demand from them allegiance to the King. If war is the alternative we can only face it, and I think that the sooner the other side is made to recognise it, the better.[41]

Griffith and Collins were furious over the warning, which they considered an unjustifiable interference with their powers. What must have been particularly galling was that when they got Childers to ask for advice on the question, none had been forthcoming. Yet when they took one of the courses outlined by Childers they were, in effect, admonished. They therefore drafted a letter, and got the whole delegation to sign it, protesting against the interference and emphasising that there would have to be a consideration of some form of association with the crown. 'Obviously,' the letter continued, 'any form of association necessitates discussion of recognition in some form or another of the head of the association.'[42]

The President was taken aback by the protest. He explained that he had not been trying to interfere with their powers as plenipotentiaries. 'There is obviously a misunderstanding,' he wrote. 'There can be no question of tying the hands of the plenipotentiaries beyond the extent to which they are tied by their original instructions. These memos of mine, except I explicitly state otherwise, are nothing more than an attempt to keep you in touch with the views of the cabinet here on the various points as they arise. I think it most important that you should be kept aware of these views.'[43]

De Valera quickly came to accept that a form of recognition would indeed be compatible with External Association. In fact, he enthusiastically endorsed the idea and eventually persuaded the other members of the cabinet to agree to recognise the King as head of the association to which Ireland would be externally linked.

Next, Griffith persuaded Lloyd George to try to end partition. If 'essential unity' were assured, the Irish chairman promised in writing he would recommend that Ireland should both accept 'free partnership with the other states associated within the British Commonwealth' and also assent to 'a recognition of the Crown as head of the proposed Association of Free States.'[44]

'The tactical course I have followed,' Griffith explained to de Valera, 'has been to throw the question of Ulster against the question of association and the Crown. This is now the position: the British Government is up against Ulster and we, for the moment, are standing aside. If they secure Ulster's consent we shall have gained "essential unity" and the difficulty we shall be up against will be the formula of association and recognition. You will observe my words, which they accept, is consistent with External Association and external recognition.'[45]

Ever since the beginning of the negotiations, de Valera explained that he had been of the opinion that if the conference were to collapse, then it would be best if the break should come on the partition question, 'provided we could so manage it that "Ulster" could not go out and cry "attachment to the Empire and loyalty to the Throne". The difficulty, of course, was to secure this without jeopardising our fundamental position.'[46]

'There can be no doubt whatever,' de Valera wrote to Griffith on 9 November 1921, 'that the delegation had managed to do this admirably.' Without formally committing themselves to anything inconsistent with External Association, the plenipotentiaries had persuaded Lloyd George to try to end partition and had apparently convinced him that he should resign rather than restart the war if Northern Ireland should refuse to accept a settlement allowing her to retain her existing autonomy within a United Ireland. In effect, Stormont would retain its powers while those powers reserved by the Westminster parliament would be transferred to a central Irish parliament.

Although there was no formal commitment to anything inconsistent with External Association, Lloyd George was nevertheless convinced that both Griffith and Collins would eventually agree to allegiance and membership of the British Commonwealth, in return for the ending of partition. It had obviously been only at the insistence of Barton, Duffy, and Childers that Griffith had made his written undertaking vague enough to keep it in line with External Association.

There was really very little indication of just what role Collins actually played in those talks, but there can be no doubt from his correspondence quoted in Rex Taylor's valuable biography that he had firmly come to the conclusion that Dominion Status was the most which could be expected for the time being, and that it should be accepted as 'a first step' towards a final settlement.[47] Yet he did not dare admit this openly at the time. Neither he nor Griffith really knew just how far they could go with those in Dublin.

'What do we accept?' Griffith asked him.

'Indeed what do we accept?' Collins wondered. He was afraid that if they accepted any British terms at all, it would be considered 'a gross betrayal or similar act of treachery.' He found that he was repeatedly asking himself why he had come to London. 'From Dublin,' he added, 'I don't know whether we're being instructed or confused. The latter I would say.'[48]

Collins felt that the only member of the delegation he could trust was Griffith, who was unfortunately ailing and would be dead within a year. At one point Griffith actually asked him to take over the real leadership of the Irish team, but they both felt the move would have to be unofficial. 'He and I recognise,' Collins wrote, 'that if such a thing were official it would provide bullets for the unmentionables.'[49] The two of them frequently discussed their apprehensions about those in Dublin.

'You realise what we have on our hands?' Griffith asked.

'I realised it long ago,' replied Collins.

'We stand or fall in this together,' said Griffith.

Collins agreed. As a youngster he had admired Griffith greatly. Now he was obviously proud to be working with him, notwithstanding the obstacles facing them. It was the one redeeming feature in the whole situation as far as he was concerned.[50]

In trying to hide his real views during the negotiations Collins gave some misleading impressions, which could later have contributed to the mistaken belief that he had changed his views radically under British pressure towards the end of the conference. On being approached during the negotiations by a nationalist delegation from Northern Ireland, for instance, he gave the distinct impression that partition would not be acceptable in any form. There was 'no principle whatever to justify' the cutting off of the Six Counties, he explained. 'In operation it would be a manifestation of the tribalistic interpretation of the principle of self-determination reducing it to an absurdity unless as originally enunciated the nation was understood as the unit — no other unit is possible in practice.'[51] He had, of course, already made it clear to the British that the Six Counties could not remain intact, but at the same time he had shown a readiness to recognise, if ultimately necessary, the partition of the area in the North East in which the Unionists had a majority.

Likewise on the allegiance question, Collins apparently tried to give the idea that he was prepared to take a firmer stand than was in fact the case. In one letter home at the beginning of the third week of the conference he certainly implied that he was not prepared to make any concession to the British on the issue. 'They'll give us *anything practically* but say they must preserve the link of the Crown,' he wrote. 'A very nominal thing is all they want.' But he indicated that he was opposed to even a nominal concession. 'Go to the devil says I in effect,' he wrote.[52]

Of course de Valera knew that Collins was leaning towards Dominion Status before he ever proposed him for the delegation, so it was particularly noteworthy that the President refused to intervene to stop the sub-conference arrangement when personally asked to do so by Duffy on 4 November and by Childers over a week later. The President was obviously satisfied that his own scheme was working admirably. After all Griffith and Collins were bringing Lloyd George closer to the Irish position, while Childers, Barton, and Duffy were preventing them from going too far, just as the President had envisaged.

The cabinet, in effect, endorsed the sub-conference set up on 13 November 1921. The cabinet meeting, which was attended by Collins and Barton — together with Duggan and Childers, who were invited to sit in on the proceedings — decided that 'whilst the utmost co-operation should exist between Dublin and London the plenipotentiaries should have a perfectly free hand but should follow original instructions re important decisions.'[53] This effectively gave the cabinet's blessing to the way things were being handled in London, seeing that Griffith and Collins had a virtual built-in majority within the five-man delegation. They could always depend on the support of Duggan, whom Barton characterised as a mere yes-man for Collins.[54]

While Collins was in Dublin for the cabinet meeting, Griffith left the British off the hook on the partition question by promising not to repudiate them if they openly suggested that a Boundary Commission be set up to redraw the border of Northern Ireland. The Irish chairman who looked on the proposal as simply helping the British to put pressure on Craig, apparently did not realise that in promising not to repudiate the proposal publicly, he was in fact agreeing to accept it, if no other solution could be agreed upon. That phase of the conference was brilliantly covered in *Peace by Ordeal* so there is no need to expand on it here, especially as

Collins was not really involved.

Griffith did report fully on his private meeting with Lloyd George. In fact, it was his longest report of the whole conference, but he did not subsequently mention that the Prime Minister afterwards had the Boundary Commission idea outlined in a memorandum which the Irish chairman nonchalantly approved when Tom Jones showed it to him the following day. Griffith attached no particular significance to the memorandum, as it only confirmed what he had discussed and already reported. He did not even mention the document to Collins, who could obviously have no objection to the Boundary Commission in principle seeing that it was he who had first suggested the idea during the plenary sessions of the conference. At the time the memorandum Griffith approved seemed to have no special significance, but it was later to play a vital role at the virtual eleventh hour when Lloyd George resurrected it with dramatic effect.

In the interim Collins argued strongly for External Association which, in line with de Valera's initial reasoning, he depicted as a means of simply ensuring that Ireland would have the same *de facto* status as that enjoyed by Canada. In support of his argument he unofficially outlined the situation for the British in a personal memorandum, which Chamberlain described as 'extraordinarily interesting though sometimes perverse and sometimes Utopian.'[55] Collins argued that:

> The only association which will be satisfactory to Ireland and to Great Britain and to the Dominions for Ireland to enter will be one based, not on the present technical legal status of the Dominions, but on the real position which they claim, and have in fact secured.
>
> In the interest of all the associated States, in the interest above all of England herself, it is essential that the present *de facto* position should be recog-

nised *de jure,* and that all its implications as regards sovereignty, allegiance, [and] constitutional independence of the governments, should be acknowledged.

Collins then went on to argue that such an association 'might form the nucleus of a real League of Nations of the world' which would afford 'the best, indeed the only possible way for England to obtain the permanent security she needs.' He felt that the United States, which had been pursuing a policy of supposed isolation following its Senate's rejection of the Versailles Treaty, might be willing to enter such a League if it was 'more fully recognised how far the claim of the Dominions to independent statehood had matured, and the progress which has been made in finding ways in which independent nations may act in concert.'[56]

In the following days Griffith and Collins made it clear they would be ready to recommend that Ireland should recognise the British King as the head of such an association. Also it was decided that the Irish would contribute to the King's revenue as a token of recognition.

On 25 November when Griffith, Collins and Barton attended the first full cabinet meeting since the beginning of the conference, Brugha took exception to the idea of contributing even a token sum. 'It is not going to settle the matter,' he said. 'I don't believe we are going to settle on that.'

Collins replied that the proposal had already been broached to the British, so de Valera appealed for unity. The President said it could be recorded that 'it had been agreed to, with one dissenting,' but this would mean that the unanimity within the cabinet for which he had been working all along would be destroyed.

'Very well,' replied Brugha, 'if it has been handed in I am agreed.' He too, wanted 'to preserve unity to the finish,' with the result that the cabinet agreed unanimously.[57]

Upon returning to London Griffith formally submitted the idea to the British along with a memorandum that covered some of the same ground as the unofficial one submitted by Collins the previous week. Contending it was fallacious to argue that Dominion Status would afford Ireland the same freedom as Canada, Griffith observed that Canada's freedom was based on the fact that she was so remote from Britain that the British could not interfere effectively in Canadian affairs but, on the other hand, they would have little difficulty in interfering in Ireland. In view of the propinquity of the two islands Griffith added, Ireland would grant the British more substantial defence concessions than the Dominions had provided but, in return, the British should recognise that 'the same propinquity imposes on us a necessity for safeguarding our independence' by insisting on External Association, which was described as a practical plan which would ensure 'Britain against every apprehension that her publicists have expressed, that will associate Ireland with her and the Dominions under the Crown, and that at the same time will secure the independence of Ireland from question or intrigue.'[58]

In essence Griffith was arguing that External Association was merely a way of ensuring that Ireland would have the same *de facto* status as the Dominions. So Lloyd George countered by offering to include in a treaty any phrase desired by the Irish 'which would ensure that the position of the Crown in Ireland should be no more in practice than it was in Canada or in any other Dominion.'

Griffith was astounded. 'With this offer,' he wrote, 'they knocked out my argument.'[59] He might just as well have written that they had undermined de Valera's own argument because the delegation had been following the

President's line of reasoning on the issue from the beginning. The Irish representatives insisted, however, that the existing oath in accordance with which members of the Canadian parliament swore to 'be faithful and bear true allegiance to King George V' needed to be revised.

The negotiations were reaching a vital stage. Next day the British revealed that they would be handing their final proposals to the Irish delegation and to Craig the following Tuesday, 6 December 1921. 'We objected,' Griffith reported. 'We should see them beforehand.'[60] They wanted the cabinet in Dublin to have a chance to see the document before Craig. The British were agreeable. It was decided that the Irish delegation would be given the proposals informally a few days in advance of being handed the document formally on 6 December.

4. Signing His Own Death Warrant

The British draft treaty, which was handed to the Irish delegation on the night of 30 November 1921, offered the Irish Free State — as Ireland would be known, the same status as the Dominions in 'law and practice'. Those exceptions, which really limited Irish freedom in comparison with the existing Dominions, were in matters of trade and defence. The British insisted on free trade and also stipulated that the coastal defence of Britain and Ireland would 'be undertaken exclusively' by the British, who would retain control of four specified ports and such other facilities as might be desired 'in times of war or of strained relations with a foreign Power.' Moreover, the size of the British and Irish armies were to be in relation to each other as each was to its country's population. Another specific difference was the form of the oath to be taken by all members of the Free State parliament. It would be one of 'allegiance to the Constitution of the Irish Free State; the Community of Nations known as the British Empire; and to the King as head of the State and of the Empire.'

On the Ulster question the draft treaty gave a fleeting recognition to Irish unity in that it applied to the whole island even though the representatives of Northern Ireland were not even consulted, but the proposals did protect their interests by stipulating that the area could opt out of the Irish Free State and decide to retain its existing status. In that event, however, a Boundary Commission would be established to adjust the boundary of Northern Ireland 'in accordance with the wishes of the inhabitants, so far as may be compatible with economic and geographic conditions.'

Keeping true to de Valera's assessment of him as 'an intellectual Republican',[1] Childers argued forcefully against the British terms, which he criticised for being too like the July proposals. He presented the delegation with an elaborate memorandum arguing that the legal and constitutional positions of the Dominions were 'two wholly different things.'[2]

Using Canada as an example, Childers pointed out that her legal status was that of 'a subordinate dependent of Britain holding her self-governing rights under a British Act of Parliament, which can legally be repealed or amended without Canada's consent.' But, he added, Canada's constitutional position was something quite different. She was an independent country in total control of her own affairs. Although the Canadians did take a direct oath of allegiance to the British Crown and were subject to the royal veto, Childers argued that 'in fact the Crown has no authority in Canada. It signifies sentiment only.' He added that 'the Canadian owes obedience to his own constitution only.' In short, he wrote, 'Canada is by the full admission of British statesmen equal in status to Great Britain and as free as Great Britain.'

Childers contended that the British had no intention of offering Ireland the same status as Canada, seeing that they were demanding certain unprecedented trade and defence concessions from the Irish. But even if those demands were dropped and the offer of complete Canadian status was made, he argued that it would only 'be illusory', because the essence of Canada's freedom was guaranteed by her distance from Britain. The British were simply too far away to enforce their legal edicts. But Ireland, on the other hand, was virtually on Britain's doorstep, so the law that distance rendered unenforceable in Canada's case, 'could be enforced against Ireland so as to over-ride the fullest constitutional freedom nominally conferred.'

Childers' memorandum, which was basically a detailed argument of de Valera's reasons for proposing External Association in the first place, was essentially the same as that put forward by Collins a week earlier and by Griffith that Monday, except Childers spelled out in much greater detail the actual freedom which Canada enjoyed. In fact, he did such a good job of outlining the Canadian position that much of what he wrote was later used to support the acceptance of the British offer guaranteeing Ireland the same *de facto* status as Canada.

Discussing the draft treaty with British leaders on 1 December, Griffith and Collins got the guarantee of *de facto* Dominion Status changed to read that the Free State would have the same status as Canada in 'law, practice and constitutional usage,' which strengthened the clause by bringing it more in line with the arguments put forward by Childers. They also objected to the oath, and Collins proposed the following alternative:

> I. . . do solemly swear to bear true faith and allegiance to the Constitution of the Irish Free State as by law established and that I will be faithful to His Majesty King George in acknowledgement of the Association of Ireland in a common citizenship with Great Britain and the group of nations known as the British Commonwealth.[3]

Such an oath would be explicitly in line with Childers' assessment of the *de facto* situation in Canada, where he contended that each 'Canadian owes obedience to his own constitution only.' The word 'faithful' was specifically included in order to denote equality between the monarch and those taking the oath, as opposed to allegiance normally owed to one's sovereign. Although the oath involved common citizenship, which was tantamount to acceptance of indirect allegiance and also membership of the British Commonwealth, the British rejected the proposal but later it was accepted with some minor alterations.

Before accepting the British terms the Irish representatives were obliged to consult the cabinet in Dublin in line with the third paragraph in their instructions. Barton and Duffy, who were opposed to the British terms, did not even want to bother going home for personal consultations, but the others insisted that the whole delegation should return for a meeting with the cabinet, as the negotiations had reached a critical stage and would have to be concluded by the following Tuesday.

Arrangements were made for a cabinet meeting at the Mansion House on Saturday morning, 3 December 1921. Griffith returned to meet de Valera on Friday night, while Collins stayed on with Childers for some talks with the British on financial matters.

At the time Collins was doing such an effective job of hiding his own attitude that Childers was at pains to understand exactly where the former stood on the British terms, which was hardly surprising as Collins had become thoroughly distrustful of Childers, whose 'advice and inspiration' he described as 'like farmland under water — dead.'[4] He and Childers set out for Dublin that evening and crossed from Holyhead on the mail boat, but it was delayed on route by an accident and did not eventually dock until shortly before the cabinet meeting convened. A sleepless night was certainly not the best preparation for the arduous meetings that were to follow.

Collins had asked for a meeting with available members of the Supreme Council of the IRB but, because of the delay, was unable to meet them as planned. Instead, he phoned Seán Ó Muirthile from the Mansion House and had him pick up a copy of the draft treaty while the cabinet was meeting.

Members of the delegation who were not in the cabinet were invited to sit in on part of the day's discussions, as were O'Higgins and Childers. Colm Ó Murchadha also attended as acting-secretary to the cabinet in the absence of Diarmuid O' Hegarty in London.

At the outset each of the plenitotentiaries gave his views on the draft terms. Griffith explained that he was in favour of accepting them, and he emphasised that he would not break on the question of the Crown. Barton, on the other hand, said the proposals were not Britain's last word, they did not really give full Dominion Status, and there was no guarantee of unity, so he was against acceptance. Gavan Duffy agreed with him, but Duggan concurred with Griffith.

There was some confusion about the attitude of Collins, who was obviously trying to show as little of his own hand as possible, especially in the presence of critics like Brugha and Stack. Childers noted in his diary that 'Collins was difficult to understand — repeatedly pressed by Dev but I really don't know what his answer amounted to.'[5] Stack later recalled that 'Collins did not speak strongly in favour of the document at all.'[6] But Ó Murchadha described him as being 'in substantial agreement' with Griffith and Duggan in arguing that rejecting the 'Treaty would be a gamble as England could arrange a war in Ireland within a week.'[7] Collins, did advocate, however, that further concessions on trade and defence could be won with pressure, and he suggested the oath should be rejected.

At the President's invitation, Childers criticised the proposals. Confining himself to the defence clauses, he denounced them saying that they meant the Free State's status would be even less than that of a Dominion. Barton asked him if the Dominions would support the

Free State in any question involving status, seeing that any British infringement in Irish affairs might be seen as setting a precedent affording Britain the right to interfere in the domestic affairs of the other Dominions.

'No,' replied Childers. So long as those defence clauses remained, he felt that the Free State would not, in effect, be a Dominion at all. 'I said,' he recalled, 'we must make it clear that we had a right to defend ourselves.' This right was being denied by the stipulation that the defence of Irish coastal waters would be undertaken 'exclusively' by Britain.[8]

When Griffith suggested that a constitutional lawyer should be consulted to interpret the significance of 'exclusively', Childers adopted a rather censorial tone. 'I said,' he wrote in his diary, 'two such lawyers had been brought by him to London and had been there for some time and could have been consulted.'

De Valera then said, according to Childers, that '"exclusively" clearly meant a prohibition on us which could not be admitted. He said he differed *from me* in that he thought it natural for them to demand facilities on our coast as being necessary. I said I didn't disagree in this but we had to keep up our principles.'

Brugha then created what Childers described as 'an unpleasant scene.' Observing that Griffith and Collins had been doing most of the negotiating, the Defence Minister asked who had been responsible for the sub-conference set up on which some of the delegation were not in complete touch with what was happening. On being told that the British had initially invited Griffith and Collins, the Defence Minister remarked that the British had selected 'their men.'

Griffith was furious. He stood up and went to where Brugha was sitting and demanded that the slanderous accusation be withdrawn, but Brugha refused at first.

Collins was angry, but he contained himself. 'If you

are not satisfied with us,' he said to Brugha, 'get another five to go over.'[9]

Barton then came to the defence of his colleagues. Notwithstanding his own dislike of the sub-conference set up, he said that Griffith and Collins had been negotiating with the 'knowledge and consent' of the full delegation.[10]

Brugha then asked that his remark be withdrawn. But the damage was already done, and an air of tension prevailed throughout the rest of the day's discussions.

The President avoided personalities in criticising the draft treaty, which he rejected mainly on the grounds that the oath was unacceptable. 'The oath,' he later wrote, 'crystallised in itself the main things we objected to — inclusion in the Empire, the British King as King of Ireland, Chief Executive of the Irish State, and the source from which all authority in Ireland was to be derived.'[11] He also criticised the fact that Northern Ireland would be allowed to vote itself out of the Irish state. While he could have understood accepting Dominion Status in return for national unity, he complained that the proposals afforded neither one nor the other, so he suggested the plenipotentiaries should return to London, try to have the document amended and, if necessary, face the consequence of war.

At one-thirty the cabinet recessed for an hour and a half, during which Collins had a hurried meeting with Ó Muirthile, who explained that their IRB colleagues had reservations about the oath, and the defence and partition provisions of the British terms. He gave Collins an alternative oath suggested by their colleagues.[12] As it was comparatively similar to the one already suggested by Collins to the British, it was not unlikely that the wording had actually been suggested by somebody who knew about the lines on which Collins was thinking.

The cabinet reconvened at three o'clock and Barton

appealed to de Valera to join the delegation on the grounds that it was unfair to ask Griffith to break on the Crown when he was unwilling to fight on the issue. The President was seriously considering the suggestion, but was reluctant to do so because, as he said himself, 'my going over would be interpreted as anxiety on our part and likely to give in. I did not want this interpretation to be placed on my action, and that extra little bit I wanted to pull them and hoped they could be pulled, could not be done if I went and therefore I was balancing these.'[13]

Griffith — who never lost an opportunity of declaring that he would not break on the issue of the Crown — emphasised his own attitude. When as many concessions as possible had been gained, he said, he would sign the agreement and go before the Dáil. That assembly was the body to decide for or against war.

'Don't you realise that, if you sign this thing, you will split Ireland from top to bottom?' Brugha interjected.

'I suppose that's so,' replied Griffith apparently struck by the implication of Brugha's words. 'I'll tell you what I'll do. I'll go back to London. I'll not sign the document, but I'll bring it back and submit it to the Dáil and, if necessary to the people.'[14]

De Valera was satisfied with the assurance. He later indicated that he would 'probably' have gone to London himself but for Griffith's undertaking not to sign the proposed treaty.[15] (It never seemed to have occurred to him that he did not have the authority to join the delegation, seeing that he had not been selected as a plenipotentiary by the Dáil as had the other members of the delegation.)

Though various defects in the British proposals were pointed out in the course of almost seven hours of discussions, the oath was the single item which evoked most criticism. In fact, with the exception of Griffith, every member of the cabinet advocated that it should be rejected. Unfortunately, Ó Murchadha's brief notes did not reflect much of the criticism. For example, he never even mentioned any of Cosgrave's contributions. But about thirty minutes before the meeting broke up, Cosgrave actually declared that he would not 'take that oath.'[16] A discussion ensued in which the cabinet was asked to suggest an alternative.

Brugha objected to having any oath at all unless the British were, in turn willing to swear to uphold the treaty. De Valera also questioned whether an oath was necessary. On being told that it was, he sought an acceptable formula to replace the oath in the draft document. 'It is obvious that you cannot have that or anything like "and the King as head of the State and the Empire",' he said. 'You could take an oath of true faith and allegiance to the Constitution of Ireland.'[17]

'I started trying to get some sort of oath,' he told the Dáil afterwards. 'Here is the oath I refer to, "I, so and so, swear to obey the Constitution of Ireland and to keep faith with His Britannic Majesty, so and so, in respect of the Treaty associating Ireland with the states of the British Commonwealth".'[18]

'Nothing doing,' declared Brugha; 'there is going to be no unanimity on such an oath as that.'[19]

'Surely Cathal,' de Valera said, 'you can't object to taking an oath if you agree to association.'[20]

Stack agreed with the President, so he, too, tried to persuade the Defence Minister that such an oath would be acceptable.

'Well,' sighed Brugha in resignation, 'you may as well swear.'[21]

'At the end of the discussion on the oath,' Childers recalled, 'I expressly raised the point myself as to whether scrapping the oath in the draft meant scrapping of the first four clauses of the British draft, that is to say the clauses setting out Dominion Status.'[22] The

President replied, 'Yes.' So Childers was satisfied. But Collins never heard the exchange.

Before the meeting concluded some decisions were taken hurriedly. It was decided that the plenipotentiaries should return to London with the same powers and instructions. If the oath was not amended, they were to reject it regardless of the consequences. If this led to a break down of the negotiations, Griffith was advised to say that the matter should be referred to the Dáil, and he was to try to put the blame on Ulster, if possible.

It was also decided that the trade and defence clauses should be amended, according to Childers, who noted that no specific suggestion was made about how to change the trade provisions. But the President did advocate that instead of the four ports they were demanding the British should be given '*two ports* only.'[23]

'All this amendment business was too hurried,' Childers noted in his diary, 'but it was understood by Barton, Duffy, and me that amendments were not mandatory on [the] delegation.' The amendments were 'only suggestions'. De Valera himself later emphasised the same point in the Dáil. 'I did not give,' he said, 'nor did the cabinet give, any instructions to the delegation as to any final document which they were to put in.'[24]

The division among the plenipotentiaries seemed deeper than ever following the cabinet meeting. The two elements of the delegation did not even return to London together. Barton, Duffy and Childers took a boat from the North Wall, while Griffith, Collins and Duggan went on the mail boat from Kingstown (Dun Laoghaire).

In his biography of Collins, Rex Taylor quoted from the record of undated exchanges between Griffith and Collins during the latter stages of the negotiations. 'I will not agree,' Collins declared, 'to anything which threatens to plunge the people of Ireland into a war — not without their authority. Still less do I agree to being dictated to by those not embroiled in these negotiations. If they are not in agreement with the steps which we are taking, and hope to take, why then did they themselves not consider their own presence here in London?' He noted, for example, that 'Brugha refused to be a member of this delegation.'

'Supposing,' Collins continued, 'we are to go back to Dublin tomorrow with a document which gave us a Republic. Would such a document find favour with everyone? I doubt it.'

'So do I,' commented Griffith. 'But sooner or later a decision will have to be made and we shall have to make it.'[25]

'There's a job to be done and for the moment here's the place,' Collins wrote to his fiancée upon his return to London. *'That's that.'*

Meanwhile Childers and Barton had begun drawing up an alternative draft treaty to the British document. They were eventually joined by Duffy. Their document included External Association, which annoyed Collins, who argued that there had been no discussion at the cabinet meeting about again seeking External Association. He was right.[26] There had been no such discussion, but the President had responded affirmatively when Childers asked if the suggested alterations to the oath also applied to the first three clauses of the British proposals. When Childers mentioned that exchange, Collins could not remember it. He was therefore understandably furious. He had thought that the cabinet had been prepared to accept the offer of *de facto* Dominion Status. Such an important issue — indeed, what would ultimately be the most vital issue — should certainly not have been determined by a simple answer to an almost throw-away question from a secretary.

Part of Collins' confusion was undoubtedly contributed to by his recollection that de Valera had proposed an oath which was consistent with Dominion Status. Together with Griffith and Duggan, he recalled that the President had suggested that in the oath they could 'recognise the King of Great Britain as Head of the Associated States.' This could be interpreted to mean that the King was being recognised as the head of each state individually as well as head of the combined association of states.

Barton and Childers, contended, however, that de Valera had proposed recognising the King only as 'Head of the Association'. Barton produced his notes of the meeting, but those were inconclusive, as he had simply written 'Head of the Assoc.' Childers, on the other hand, actually recorded in his diary that the President had suggested 'King of the Associated States.'[27] Moreover, Ó Murchadha's notes were identical with the version remembered by Griffith, Collins and Duggan.

When de Valera later contended that he had said 'Association' not 'Associated States,' he found himself in the embarrassing position of confronting formidable evidence. He actually damaged his own case during a secret session of the Dáil on 16 December by recalling what he had said a fortnight earlier.

'I do swear to recognise the King of Great Britain as Head of the Associated States,' he said. 'That is the way I expressed it verbally meaning the association of states.'[28]

As this form of the oath was rejected by the British, it is not really of importance here except that the whole controversy surrounding it does help to illustrate why Collins could have wondered whether Dublin was trying to advise or confuse the delegation. He was actually so annoyed over the confusion about re-proposing External Association that he seemed to adopt obstructionist tactics in criticising the defence provisions of the intended counter proposals, according to Childers, who felt that Collins 'deliberately' tried to make the new document 'unreasonable' by insisting that 'Dev had said that only two ports [and] nothing else', could be conceded to the British.[29]

Notwithstanding his position as only a secretary, Childers had no compunction about arguing with, or criticising, the deputy leader of the delegation. 'I protested against making Dev's words ridiculous,' Childers noted in his diary.

Griffith, Collins and Duggan initially refused to present the counter proposals to the British on the grounds that it would only be a waste of time, seeing the British had already rejected External Association on numerous occasions. Barton and Duffy accepted the challenge, and Griffith then agreed to go with them to Downing Street, but Collins and Duggan refused. 'I did not attend this conference,' Collins wrote next day, 'for the reason that I had, in my own estimation, argued fully all points.'[30] Moreover, he had already shown that he was prepared to accept *de facto* Dominion Status by proposing an oath which was consistent with Irish membership of the British Commonwealth.

The British again flatly rejected External Association, as Collins predicted. The meeting actually broke up when Duffy blurted out that the Irish 'difficulty is coming into the Empire'. At that point the whole conference broke down. The two sides announced they would submit their final proposals the following day and would then formally announce that the conference had collapsed.

There followed a rather strained meeting of the Irish delegates in Childers' room at Han's Place. When Griffith read out his report of the sub-conference meeting, Barton called for the inclusion of a complaint by Lloyd George to the effect that the Irish counter proposals 'were a complete going back on the discussions of the last week of so.' Collins protested strongly that this implied that Griffith and himself had been giving way to the British.[31]

Duffy supported Barton, who held his ground and read out the note he had taken of the remark during the actual meeting. But instead of the word, 'on', that note had the word, 'upon', which Griffith and Collins accepted. They felt that, so worded, Lloyd George's remark merely referred to the latest document as a re-hash of amendments discussed and rejected the previous week.

The distrust within the Irish delegation was so strong that each element felt the other was trying to blame it for the collapse of the negotiations. Duffy and Barton were particularly dispondent. They privately told Childers that Griffith had 'made fools' of them by jockeying them into the position in which they seemed responsible for the break up of the conference.

While Childers was typing up the report for the cabinet in Dublin, Griffith instructed him to include mention that the British had suggested the 'possibility of *"changing the form of the oath".'* The chairman explained he had forgotten to mention that point earlier. Neither Barton nor Duffy were available at the time, so Childers included the material, but he checked with the others before allowing the report to be dispatched.

Barton agreed to the inclusion, even though he could not remember anything being said about the matter, but Duffy did remember. He recalled that Birkenhead had remarked rather casually that the oath could be changed. If the difficulties in drawing up the report of that sub-conference meeting — which was the only one attended by both Barton and Duffy — were anything to go on, then it was little wonder that Griffith and Collins had been anxious to exclude them from the actual talks. But, of course, by then the atmosphere within the delegation had been poisoned by the distrust brought on by the whole sub-conference set up.

Although the conference had, in effect, broken down, Tom Jones tried to salvage the situation that night. He had a private meeting with Griffith, whom he found 'labouring under a deep sense of the crisis.' The Irish chairman 'spoke thoughout with the greatest earnestness and unusual emotion.' He explained that Collins and himself were in favour of the British terms, but needed something further to offer the Dáil. Their position would be simplified, he said, if the British could get Craig to give 'a conditional recognition, however shadowy, of Irish national unity in return for the acceptance of the Empire by Sinn Féin.'[32]

If the British delegation could obtain an assurance that Northern Ireland would agree to unity, Griffith said Dublin would give all the safeguards that the Northern majority needed and would even agree to scrapping the Boundary Commission. With a Northern guarantee of unity, he was confident he could get the Dáil to accept a treaty containing an oath which would be acceptable to the British. He added that Barton and the doctrinaire Republicans could then be ignored, because ninety per cent of the gun-men would follow Collins.

Without the support of Collins, however, Griffith did not have a chance of getting the Dáil to accept the British terms. He therefore asked Jones to arrange a meeting so that Lloyd George could have a 'heart to heart' talk with Collins. Jones then left and arranged the meeting with the Prime Minister for the following morning, but Griffith had great difficulty in persuading Collins to attend.

The latter was still so annoyed over the confusion caused by the cabinet meeting in Dublin that he was refusing to have anything further to do with the negotiations. It was not until just before the meeting with Lloyd George was due to take place that he finally relented and agreed to go to Downing Street. He had, in fact, been so determined not to attend that he was about a quarter of an hour late for the meeting, which was most uncharacteristic as he had a virtual obsession about punctuality.

During the meeting Collins emphasised that he was 'perfectly dissatisfied' with the British terms regarding Northern Ireland. He said the British government should get the position clarified by pressing Craig for a letter either accepting unity under certain specified conditions, of flatly rejecting it. According to Collins, the Prime Minister remarked that:

> I myself pointed out on a previous occasion that the North would be forced economically to come in. I assented but I said the position was so serious owing to certain recent actions that for my part I was anxious to secure a definite reply from Craig and his colleagues, and that I was as agreeable to a reply rejecting as accepting. In view of the former we would save Tyrone and Fermanagh, parts of Derry, Armagh and Down by the Boundary Commission, and thus avoid such things as the raid on the Tyrone County Council and the ejection of the staff. Another such incident would, in my view, inevitably lead to a conflict, and this conflict, in the nature of things (assuming for instance that some of the Anglo-Northern police were killed or wounded) would inevitably rapidly spread throughout Ireland. Mr Lloyd George expressed a view that this might be put to Craig, and if so the safeguards would be a matter for working out between ourselves and Craig afterwards.[33]

The Prime Minister was willing to consider some objections to the financial, trade and defence clauses of the British draft treaty. he also said that he would consider a new oath, if the Irish delegation accepted the clauses concerning Dominion Status.

'Finally,' Collins concluded his report, 'the conversation developed into a statement by Mr Lloyd George to the effect that were Clauses 1 and 2 accepted he would be in a position to hold up any action until we had, if we desired to do so, submitted the matter to Dáil Éireann and the country. I left it at that saying that unless I sent word to the contrary some members of the delegation would meet him at 2 o'clock.' Arrangements were then made for the members of the two delegations to meet that afternoon.

This time Barton accompanied Griffith and Collins, and they met with the Prime Minister, Chamberlain, Birkenhead and Churchill. From the outset Griffith tried to concentrate on the Ulster question by demanding that the Irish delegation should know whether Craig would accept or reject Irish unity. The British countered that Griffith was going back on his previous promise not to let them down on the Boundary Commission proposal.

'Collins said,' according to Barton, 'that for us to agree to any conditions defining the future relations of Great Britain and Ireland prior to Craig's giving his assent to the unity of Ireland was impossible, that to do so would be to surrender our whole fighting position. That every document we ever sent them had stated that any proposals for the association of Ireland with the British Commonwealth of Nations was conditional upon the unity of Ireland. That, unless Craig accepted inclusion under the all-Ireland Parliament, the unity of Ireland was not assured and that if he refused inclusion we should be left in the position of having surrendered our position without having even secured the essential unity of Ireland.'[34]

Lloyd George became excited and accused the Irish delegation of trying to break off the talks on the Ulster question when the real difficulty was the opposition of those in Dublin to membership of the Empire. He accused Griffith of breaking the earlier promise concerning the Boundary Commission, and he produced the memorandum that the Irish chairman had assented to back in mid-November.

'What is this letter?' Barton whispered to Collins.

'I don't know what the hell it is,' growled the latter.

'Do you mean to tell me, Mr Collins, that you never learnt of this document from Mr Griffith?'[35]

The memorandum outlining the Boundary Commission proposal was then passed across the table to Collins and Barton, both of whom were seeing it for the first time. But Collins said nothing.

The Prime Minister explained that he had assumed Griffith had told Collins about the memorandum, so the two of them were therefore a party to it. 'I have fulfilled my part of the bargain,' Lloyd George continued. 'I took the risk of breaking my party. You in Ireland often bring against us in England the charge of breach of faith. Now it is for you to show that Irishmen know how to keep faith.'[36]

'I said I would not let you down on that, and I won't,' Griffith declared.[37] He no longer felt able to hold out on the Ulster question, but he argued that it was unfair to hold the rest of the Irish delegation to his private promise.

The discussion changed to other subjects, and the British agreed to an oath introduced by Collins that morning with only some minor verbal changes. They also agreed to other verbal concessions, such as dropping the stipulation that the British would have the *exclusive* right to defend the seas around Ireland and adding a clarification to the effect that the clause did 'not prevent the construction or maintenance by the Government of the Irish Free State of such vessels as are necessary for the protection of the Revenue or the Fisheries.' It was further provided that the whole defence question would be reviewed by the two governments in five years 'with a view to the undertaking by Ireland of a share in her own coastal defence.' Lloyd George then offered one further major concession. If the Irish delegation would agree to the British terms, he would drop the demand for free trade.

Griffith replied that he would sign the agreement but added it was unfair to ask his colleagues to do so before they knew where Craig stood on the proposals.

'Do I understand, Mr Griffith, that though everyone else refuses, you will nevertheless agree to sign?' Lloyd George asked.

'Yes, that is so, Mr Prime Minister.'[38]

'That is not enough,' Lloyd George said quickly; 'if we sign; we shall sign as a delegation and stake the life of the Government on our signature. Is the Irish delegation prepared to do the same?' As Griffith had not only agreed to sign already but had also told Jones the previous night that Collins was in favour of Britain's terms, it was obvious Barton was the one the British had now to convince as the Prime Minister proceeded to issue his infamous ultimatum.

'He particularly addressed himself to me.' Barton reported, 'and said very solemnly that those who were not for peace must take the full responsibility for the war that would immediately follow refusal by any delegate to sign the Articles of Agreement.'[39]

'I have to communicate with Sir James Craig tonight,' Lloyd George said as he raised two envelopes. 'Here are the alternative letters which I have prepared, one enclosing the Articles of Agreement reached by His Majesty's government and yourselves, and the other saying that Sinn Féin representatives refuse the oath of allegiance and refuse to come within the Empire. If I send this letter, it is war — and war within three days! Which letter am I to send?[40] Whichever letter you choose travels by special train to Holyhead, and by destroyer to Belfast. The train is waiting with steam up at Euston. Mr Shakespeare is ready. If he is to reach Sir James Craig in time we must have your answer by ten p.m. tonight. You can have until then, but no longer to decide whether you will give peace or war to your country.'[41]

The Irish delegation withdrew to consider its next move. 'Michael Collins rose looking as though he was going to shoot someone,' according to Churchill. 'I have never seen so much pain and suffering in restraint.'

Realising that the talks had come to a vital stage, in view of Craig's announcement that he would have Britain's final terms or else the conference would have broken down by the following day, the press were waiting anxiously in Downing Street. As Collins left the Prime Minister's residence, he was asked if the Irish delegation would be returning later that evening.

'I don't know,' he replied.

'Has the conference finished?'

'I don't know that either.'[42]

On the way to their headquarters, however, Collins told Barton of his intention to sign. The surprise with which the latter greeted the decision testified to the skilful way in which Collins had concealed his real views in recent weeks. Although Duggan was also in favour of signing, Barton and Duffy held out for a time.

The problem, according to Griffith, was to decide, 'Would we, or would we not, come within the Community of Nations known as the British Empire?'[43] The moment of truth had come. They were plenipotentiaries and they had to make the decision themselves. Nobody even thought of telephoning Dublin, according to Barton, nor did anyone mention the undertaking which Griffith gave to Brugha might have obliged them not to sign.

Griffith 'spoke almost passionately for signing,' according to Childers, who noted that Collins said virtually nothing during the argument, which was 'long and hot'. On three occasions Griffith, Collins and Duggan were 'on the point of proceeding to sign' without the others but Barton stalled them.[44] The argument went on for so long that the delegation was still at Han's Place more than an hour after the time limit set by Lloyd George had expired.

When eleven o'clock passed without a sign of the Irish representatives returning, the British became uneasy. 'We had doubts as to whether we would see them again,' the Prime Minister recalled afterwards.[45]

He realised that much depended on Collins. 'If only Michael Collins has as much moral courage as he has physical courage,' Lloyd George said, 'we shall get a settlement. But moral courage is a much higher quality than physical courage, and it is a quality that brave men often lack.'[46]

Collins had already made it clear to the other members of the Irish delegation that he took a bleak view of the IRA's prospects of success if the fighting should be restarted. He was convinced it would not be possible to attain further success by physical force and his own effectiveness as intelligence chief was ended, seeing that his agents within Dublin Castle had been uncovered. In addition, he would not be able to move about Dublin with the same ease as he had before the Truce because he was now well-known to the British who would have little difficulty in recognising him.

'He knew that physical resistance, if resumed, would collapse and he was not going to be the leader of a forlorn hope,' Barton explained years later. 'He intended to live to fight again.'[47] At one point in the discussion at Han's Place, Collins pointed out that there had been only 2,000 active volunteers, and he asked if Barton wished to send them out to be slaughtered.

'Barton,' said Duggan 'you will be hanged from a lamp post in the streets of Dublin if your refusal to sign causes a new war in Ireland.'[48]

Barton was shaken. He did not place much weight in Duggan's opinion, but he did feel that 'Collins was in a better position to appraise our military position than anyone else.' He therefore asked to be allowed to consult privately with Childers.

It seemed de Valera's belief that Childers would be able to hold Barton in line was correct. When the two of them were alone, Barton asked for the advice of his cousin, who promptly urged him to hold out as it was a matter of principle. Childers added that his own wife Molly, would agree with them.

'Well,' said Barton, apparently irritated that Childers should be judging the situation by what his American wife would think, 'I suppose I must sign.' He then returned and announced his decision to sign, and Duffy followed suit.[49]

In the last analysis, therefore, de Valera had miscalculated in thinking Childers would keep Barton in line, because he not only failed to do so but actually helped drive him over it. Next day Barton told Childers privately that the 'allusion to Molly's support for refusal to sign last night' had been the 'deciding element' in his decision to sign. Nevertheless Childers still believed the main factor had been Barton's 'belief that war was really imminent and inevitable — real war.'[50] In other words, the remark about Molly Childers had only been the proverbial straw that broke the camel's back.

Much has been written about Lloyd George's insistence that the pressing need to notify Craig did not allow sufficient time for the Irish delegation to refer the final draft of the Treaty back to Dublin before the signing. Geoffrey Shakespeare, who was waiting to take the message to Craig, later wrote that he 'never understood why the Irish accepted the ultimatum at its face value. Why did they not call the bluff?'[51]

Griffith and Collins must have known the story about Craig was only part of a bluff, because they knew that Lloyd George had initially planned to present Britain's final terms to Craig at the same time they were to be given to the Irish delegation on 6 December 1921. The British apparently intended to follow the same procedure as had been followed in 1919 with the Versailles Treaty, which had been given to the German delegation and published some weeks before it was actually signed. Griffith and Collins had insisted, however, that the cabinet in Dublin should be allowed to see the terms before Craig, so the document was then given to them early. Consequently they must have known that Lloyd George's schedule simply called for the British to forward a copy of their final terms to Craig — not necessarily have an agreement signed by that date. Indeed the Prime Minister actually told Collins that morning he would allow the Treaty to be referred back to the Dáil before signing, if the Irish delegation were prepared to recommend Dominion Status.

Although Shakespeare thought the insistence that the Irish delegates should sign that night was part of a bluff, this did not mean that he believed they could have won further concessions, as has been inferred. 'Lloyd George was not bluffing in refusing further concessions,' Shakespeare wrote. 'He had gone to the limit, and there was nothing more to offer.' The Prime Minister was afraid, however, that if the 'Irish delegates went back without signing or expressing an opinion, the atmosphere in Dublin would have influenced them and the Treaty would have been lost.'[52] Hence the ultimatum.

In Griffith's case, of course, the ultimatum was insignificant. He had agreed to sign before it was issued. It would have been completely out of character for Collins to have deserted his colleague at that stage. He had already agreed that the two of them were in the negotiations together to the bitter end.

But Collins did not explain to Barton that he thought 'the threat of immediate and terrible war was probably bluff.'[53] Instead, he and Griffith went along with the bluff, possibly in order to ensure that all of their colleagues signed, as this would make it easier to get the agreement accepted in Dublin. Without Barton's vote, for example, they would have little chance of getting the cabinet to accept the Treaty, as they realised that de Valera, Brugha and Stack would be opposed. If Barton joined that trio, then the majority of the cabinet would be opposed to the British terms and the Dáil might not be given any more say than it had been given with the July proposals, which were formally rejected before the Dáil even convened to discuss them.

Having been entrusted by the Dáil with the responsibility of negotiating an acceptable settlement, Griffith and Collins saw it as their duty to sign when they were convinced that the terms would be acceptable not only to a majority of Dáil deputies but also a majority of the Irish people. Moreover, they thought that an unwinable war would inevitably follow their refusal to agree to a settlement.

'Unquestionably, the alternative to the Treaty, sooner or later, was war,' Collins later wrote. 'To me it would have been a criminal act to refuse to allow the Irish nation to give its opinion as to whether it would accept this settlement or resume hostilities.'[54]

Some notes which Collins drew up during the latter stages of the London conference give a clear insight into his thinking. He was convinced that Ireland would benefit from Dominion Status, which he did not consider *'as being anywhere near a finalised solution. It is the first step,'* he wrote. *'More than this could not be expected.'*[55]

'I am never of the opinion that the majority of the Irish people will be against such a Treaty as we have in mind,' he observed in another note. 'It is a question of greater influence — de Valera will command, I think, a large part of what was formerly the Volunteer Organisation.' Believing that there would be opposition in Dublin from 'those who have in mind personal ambitions under pretence of patriotism' Collins still thought that fifty-five to sixty per cent 'of all concerned' would support the Treaty.[56] It was therefore clear to him where his duty lay, and he signed in the full knowledge of the likely consequences for himself.

Immediately after signing, for example, Birkenhead turned to Collins and said, 'I may have signed my political death-warrant tonight.'

'I may have signed my actual death-warrant,' was the young Irishman's sombre reply.[57]

Within minutes the Irish delegates emerged from Number 10 Downing Street looking very tired and grave.

'Have you anything to say?' a reporter asked Collins.

'Not a word,' he replied sharply.[58]

Collins was obviously deeply troubled. Some hours later he wrote a truly prophetic letter to a friend:

> Think — what have I got for Ireland? Something which she has wanted these past seven hundred years. Will anyone be satisfied at the bargain? Will anyone? I tell you this early this morning I signed my death warrant. I thought at the time how odd, how

ridiculous — a bullet may just as well have done the job five years ago.

I believe Birkenhead may have said an end to his political life. With him it has been my honour to work.

These signatures are the first real step for Ireland. If people will only remember that — the first real step.[59]

5. Between Ghosts and Reality: The Treaty Debate

'In the creation of the Irish Free State we have laid a foundation on which may be built a new world order,' Collins explained to an Associated Press correspondent on the day the Treaty was signed. But if the young Irishman believed what he was contending, then one could only conclude that he had little appreciation of the existing international political situation. Just because Ireland was supposedly being accorded *de facto* Dominion Status was certainly absurd grounds for thinking that the British Commonwealth would now be a League of Free Nations in which even the United States would be prepared to participate. Yet, arguing on the lines of the memorandum he had submitted to the British while pressing for External Association a few weeks earlier, Collins now declared that 'Ireland would be a link to join America and Britain. And with America in this League of Free Nations, what country would wish to stay outside?'[1]

De Valera's initial reaction on hearing that a treaty had been signed was one of delight. Because of Griffith's promise not to sign the draft treaty the previous Saturday, the President assumed that the British must have conceded External Association.

'I never thought that they would give in so soon,' he remarked to those with him.[2]

It was only that evening as he was about to attend a cultural gathering that Eamon Duggan and Desmond Fitzgerald arrived from London with a copy of the Treaty, which Duggan handed to the President. When the latter showed no interest in the document, Duggan asked him to read it.

'What should I read it for?' de Valera asked.

'It is arranged that the thing be published in London and Dublin simultaneously at 8 o'clock and it is near that hour now,' replied Duggan.

'What,' said the President, 'to be published whether I have seen it or not?'

'Oh well, that's the arrangement.'[3]

De Valera was despondent with the terms of the Treaty. He summoned a meeting of the available members of the cabinet the following morning and revealed that he intended to demand the resignations of Griffith, Collins and Barton from his government upon their return, but he was dissuaded from taking any final decision by Cosgrave, who argued that the plenipotentiaries should personally be allowed to explain what had happened in London. A full cabinet meeting was therefore called for the following day 8 December 1921, and a press release was prepared announcing that 'in view of the nature of the proposed treaty with Great Britain, President de Valera has sent an urgent summons to members of the cabinet in London to report at once so that a full cabinet decision may be taken.'

Desmond Fitzgerald, the Minister for Publicity, was surprised at the tone of the release. 'This might be altered, Mr President,' he said entering the cabinet room. 'It reads as if you were opposed to the settlement.'

'And that is the way I intend it to read,' replied de Valera. 'Publish it as it is.'

'I did not think he was against this kind of settlement before we went over to London,' the amazed Fitzgerald whispered to Stack.

'He is dead against it *now* anyway,' replied Stack. 'That's enough.'[4]

Looking on the remark as a cry of triumph, Fitzgerald

thought Stack was gloating that he and Brugha had persuaded the President to abandon his more moderate views while the plenipotentiaries were in London. In view of de Valera's moderate pronouncements not only in the months leading up to the truce, but especially during the summer when he made it clear that he was no doctrinaire Republican, many people concluded that he would be in favour of the terms of the Treaty. After all, the plenipotentiaries had gone to London with the aim of securing 'the status of a Dominion' and they had returned with what was essentially Dominion Status. Some people were even convinced that Collins expected the President's support, but this was not the case. He realised that de Valera would oppose the agreement, if only on selfish grounds. Thus Collins' first question upon his return home was to ask Tom Cullen, one of his intelligence men, how his own people viewed the Treaty.

'Tom,' he said, 'what are our fellows saying?'

'What is good enough for you is good enough for them,' replied Cullen.[5]

Yet there were already some ominous signs. The previous evening in London the delegation was given such a tumultuous send off by Irish exiles that Childers actually wrote in his diary that he was 'nearly crushed to death.'[6] So Collins found it 'in a sense prophetic' that there was no welcoming crowd and 'no signs of jubilation' on reaching Dublin next morning. Instead, the few people who were about 'seemed strangely apathetic.'[7]

'This lack of jubilation among the people was dispiriting enough,' Collins continued, 'but it was nothing compared with the open hostility we faced in the cabinet drawing room of the Mansion House.' De Valera was waiting there looking gaunt and depressed, while Stack was in a blazing mood and Brugha was 'the personification of venom'.

The ensuing cabinet meeting, which recessed three times, lasted through the afternoon and into the late evening. The merits and disadvantages of the Treaty were examined, but not in any great detail, according to Stack, who recalled that the main topic of discussion was the circumstances under which the plenipotentiaries had signed the agreement. Griffith refused to 'admit duress by the British,' which was, of course, accurate in his case seeing that he had agreed to sign before Lloyd George issued his infamous ultimatum. Collins, on the other hand, said that 'if there was duress it was only "the duress of the facts".'[8]

'I did not sign the Treaty under duress,' he later wrote, 'except in the sense that the position as between Ireland and England, historically, and because of superior forces on the part of England, has always been one of duress.' He added, 'there was not, and could not have been, any personal duress.'[9] But both Barton and Duffy stated that they had been intimidated into signing.

Of course nobody contended that Lloyd George had attempted coercion in the sense of physically threatening anyone. 'The form of duress he made use of,' according to Barton, 'was a more insidious and in my opinion, a more compelling duress, for Mr Lloyd George, knowing already from Mr Griffith himself that he was prepared to sign, demanded that every other delegate should sign or war would follow immediately, and insisted that those who refused to sign must accept the responsibility.' To Barton's mind this meant that he would have to act against the wishes of the majority of his own delegation and 'accept the personal responsibility for the slaughter to ensue' without having a chance 'to consult the President, the cabinet in Dublin, the Dáil, or the people.' Thus under the circumstances he decided to sign.[10]

Barton actually blamed de Valera for the mess. The President, he said, had vacillated from the beginning and had even refused to go to London when asked that weekend. The problem was, Barton declared, '*We were not a fighting delegation.*'[11]

Had it not been for Griffith's undertaking not to sign the Treaty, the President said that he would have gone to London himself and rejected the British terms. 'I *would* have gone and said, "Go to the devil. I will not sign".'[12]

The cabinet voted to endorse the Treaty by the narrowest margin possible. Griffith, Collins and Cosgrave lined up in favour, while the President, Brugha and Stack were in opposition. It was therefore Barton's vote which made the difference. Even though he was personally opposed to the agreement, he explained that he felt bound to vote for it, seeing he had already signed it and agreed to recommend it to the Dáil. Had he not signed therefore, it was likely that the Treaty would have been rejected by the cabinet, and the Dáil might have had no more say in the matter than with the British proposals that July.

Kevin O'Higgins, who did not have a vote in the cabinet, said that while the Treaty should never have been signed, it should be supported as it was important to preserve a united front. Diarmuid O'Hegarty, the cabinet secretary, then interrupted with a strong appeal to the President not to oppose the Treaty, but Childers called for a protest in the Dáil against 'the irrevocable step of signing away independence.'[13]

De Valera spoke 'at great length'. Although repeatedly pressed, he rejected the suggestion that he not speak out publicly. He explained he had been working for unity by seeking a form of association which people like Brugha and Stack could accept, but all that had been thrown away without the permission of the cabinet. However, 'he did not despair of winning better terms yet,' according to Childers, who found privately that the President seemed 'certain of winning'.[14]

An effort was made to persuade the plenipotentiaries 'not to press the document on the Dáil.' At one point Stack appealed to Collins personally. 'You have signed and undertaken to recommend the document to the Dáil,' he said. 'Well, recommend it. Your duty stops there. You are not supposed to throw all your influence into the scale.' If the agreement was rejected, he argued they would be in an even stronger position than before. 'Will you do it?' Stack asked.

But Collins contemptuously dismissed the suggestion. 'Where would I be then?' he snarled.[15]

The cabinet was irrevocably split. De Valera announced he would resign if the Treaty were accepted, while both Griffith and Collins said that they would do the same if it were rejected. In the interim, however, it was decided that all should carry on until the Dáil could vote on the agreement.

Following the meeting de Valera issued a statement to the press complaining that 'the terms of the agreement are in violent conflict with the wishes of the majority of the nation.' But he added there was 'a definite constitutional way of resolving our political differences.'

Though the first obstacle on the road towards ratification had been overcome, Collins was obviously troubled after the meeting. He called at Batt O'Connor's home, where he had been a frequent visitor during the terror, but now he was unsure of his welcome. When O'Connor opened the door, Collins did not walk in as usual but stood there on the doorstep 'with a strange expression' on his face.[16]

'Come in,' said the somewhat puzzled O'Connor. 'What are you waiting for?'

'I thought you would have no welcome for me, Batt,'

replied Collins. He was, of course, welcome, but he was so disturbed by the cabinet meeting that he was unable to relax. Too agitated to sit down, he strode around the room, gesturing animatedly with his hands flaying the air in a deep emotional display. Should the Treaty be defeated he said that he would move back down the country.

'I will leave Dublin at once,' Collins said bitterly. 'I will go down to Cork. If the fighting is going to be resumed, I will fight in the open, beside my own people down there. I am not going to be chivvied and hunted through Dublin as I have been for the last two years.

O'Connor argued that the Irish people should be allowed to have a say on the Treaty. 'You have brought back this Treaty,' he said. 'It is a wonderful achievement. The people want it. They must at least be given the chance to say what they think of it. Then if they reject it (only they will not reject it) you will have done your part, and will have no responsibility for the consequences.'

Collins agreed that the Irish people should have their say. 'I will accept their verdict,' he declared.

When the Supreme Council of the IRB met to consider the Treaty two days later, Collins chaired the meeting at which Liam Lynch raised the only dissenting voice. The latter was sorry that he felt compelled to differ with Collins but felt his opposition would not strain their friendship. 'I admire Mick as a soldier and a man,' Lynch wrote. 'Thank God all parties can agree to differ.'[17]

The Supreme Council endorsed the Treaty but announced that all Dáil deputies would have 'freedom of action in the matter'. Thus the IRB determined to make no effort to compel its members to vote for ratification.[18]

There was a great air of anticipation on 14 December 1921 as the Dáil convened in a hall of University College at Earlsfort Terrace, Dublin. It was significant that the division within the cabinet manifested itself at the outset in the seating arrangements which saw de Valera, Brugha and Stack positioned to the left of the Speaker, while Griffith, Collins and the other members of the delegation took up their seats across the floor. Most members of the general body sat facing the Speaker, with the public gallery behind them, while more than one hundred journalists from around the world were crammed together at the other end of the hall behind the Speaker's chair.

A motion to go into private session was supposed to have been introduced following the roll call, but de Valera rose to speak first. It was but a foretaste of what was to come during the following days. Whenever the President wanted to say something he seemed to act almost as if he had a right to determine his own procedure. During thirteen days of public and private debate, he interrupted the proceedings more than 250 times. It was, no doubt, evidence of the enormous respect with which he was held in the Dáil that he was allowed to interrupt so often. Admittedly many of those interruptions were little more than brief interjections, but some were quite lengthy. Excluding his formal speech against the Treaty, for example, his contributions actually took up over thirty-nine pages in the official reports, in comparision to similar contributions of twelve pages by Collins and only eight by Griffith.[19]

By any standards the President's initial remarks were an inauspicious introduction to such an historical occasion. Speaking in Irish he explained that, as his command of the language was not as good as he would like and as it was easier for him to gather his thoughts in English, he would therefore speak in English. But on breaking into English, he gave an entirely different reason for not continuing in Gaelic. 'Some members,' he said, 'do not know Irish, I think, and consequently what I shall say will be in English.'*

The President was almost casual as he stood there with one hand by his side and three pages of typewritten notes in the other as he went on to disassociate himself from the actions of those who had signed the Treaty. He admitted that the members of the delegation had been given full plenipotentiary powers with the right to differ from the cabinet. 'If there was any difference of opinion,' he said, 'the plenipotentiaries had the responsibility of making up their own minds and deciding on it.' Nevertheless the delegation had been issued with secret instructions, which he revealed for the first time. Those had been observed, he added, with the exception of the understanding in the third paragraph in accordance with which the plenipotentiaries should have submitted 'the complete text of a draft treaty about to be signed' and should have awaited a reply from the cabinet before signing.

Contending that the plenipotentiaries knew he would not accept the Treaty, de Valera admitted that they acted 'in accordance with their rights' when they decided to sign anyway. 'As far as relations between the cabinet and the plenipotentiaries are concerned,' he added, 'the only point is that paragraph three was not carried out to the letter.' He therefore suggested the whole issue 'should not in any way interfere with the discussion on the Treaty which the plenipotentiaries have brought to us. We are to treat it on its merits.'

De Valera then changed the subject to the question of a private session from which the press and public would be excluded. He wanted such a session so that he could

---

* The President had begun:
'Tá fhios againn go léir cé an fáth go bhfuilimíd anseo iniu agus an cheist mhór atá againn le socrú. Níl mo chuid Gaedhilge chó maith agus ba mhaith liom í bheith. Is fearr is féidir liom mo smaointe do nochtadh as Beurla, agus dá bhrí sin is dóich liom gurbh fearra dhom labairt as Beurla ar fad.

introduce his alternative document in the hope of getting it accepted in place of the Treaty, though he did not explain this publicly at the time. He simply indicated that it would be best to answer questions regarding the differences between the cabinet and the plenipotentiaries in a private session.

Both Griffith and Collins were unwilling to allow the subject to be changed so easily. If the President had not wished to make an issue of their signing, he should not have brought up the question in the first place.

Collins adamantly refuted any suggestion that the plenipotentiaries had exceeded their authority or violated their instructions. For one thing they had only assented to a document, which, he emphasised, they 'did not sign as a treaty, but did sign on the understanding that each signatory would recommend it to the Dáil for acceptance.' The document, which was officially headed 'Articles of Agreement for a Treaty between Great Britain and Ireland' would not in effect, become a treaty until it had been ratified.

In order that the circumstances surrounding the signing could be fully understood, Collins wanted the fullest possible disclosure of documents relating to the negotiations in London. He was therefore annoyed when the President acted selectively in reading the secret instructions given to the plenipotentiaries without even mentioning the credentials conferred on them at the same time. Standing with hands in pockets, Collins began speaking slowly but firmly. While sitting there, one reporter noted, his eyes had glimmered softly, but now that he was aroused, they narrowed and became intense.

'If one document had to be read,' Collins said with his jaw set determinedly and his voice vibrant with the intensity of his feelings, 'the original document, which was a prior document, should have been read first.

I must ask the liberty of reading the original document which was served on each member of the delegation.'

'Is that the one with the original credentials?' de Valera asked.

'Yes,' replied Collins.

'Was that ever presented?' asked the President. 'It was given in order to get the British Government to recognise the Irish Republic. Was that document giving the credentials of the accredited representatives from the Irish Government presented to, or accepted by, the British delegates? Was that seen by the British delegates or accepted by them?'

It was a dramatic moment as de Valera stood there facing Collins across the floor. Then Collins turned to the Speaker and paused momentarily. 'May I ask,' he said calmly, almost jocularly, 'that I be allowed to speak without interruption?'.

'I must protest,' the President insisted. But the Speaker called for order and de Valera sat down.

Collins then continued. With dramatic effect he read the credentials signed by the President himself. Those specifically authorised the plenipotentiaries 'to negotiate and conclude' a treaty with Britain. He did not stress the word 'conclude', but the reading of the terms of reference seemed to create a profound impression on all those present in the hall.

From his 'slow, measured tones', Collins gradually built himself into 'a crescendo of anger and indignation' as he repeated that the credentials should have been read along with the insturctions so that members of the Dáil would be in a position to judge the issue properly. In order that the issue would not be prejudged, he stated he had refrained from trying to influence members of the Dáil beforehand, although he knew that he was being villified himself. 'I have not said a hard word about anyone,' he emphasised as he rapped the table in front of him. 'I have been called a traitor.'

'By whom?' de Valera asked immediately, possibly thinking that he was being accused of making the charge himself.

The atmosphere was electric as Collins ignored the question. 'If there are men who act towards me as a traitor I am prepared to meet them any where, any time, now as in the past,' he declared. Murmurs spread throughout the room. De Valera sat staring at Collins while ministers and deputies became restless. But then the tension dissipated as Collins changed the subject and continued in a more ordinary tone. Even though he was opposed to a private session, he explained he would accept one.

'If there is anything, any matter of detail, if, for instance, the differences as they arose from time to time, should be discussed first in private, I am of the opinion that having discussed it in private, I think we ought then to be able to make it public,' he said. 'I am willing to go as far as that, that is only detail. But on the essentials I am for publicity now and all along.' In short, he was prepared to discuss the differences in private so that misunderstandings might be cleared up, but the deputies should then be free to explain their own points of view.

The debate drifted as various members argued whether or not to go into private session. Although de Valera wanted one, Brugha — demonstrating that sincerity and independence which even Collins admired — objected. Then suddenly the President revived the controversy over the credentials by charging that Collins had earlier wished 'to lay stress on the word "conclude".'

'No, sir,' said Collins emphatically. He had already made it quite clear that the Dáil was free to reject the agreement. Yet de Valera persisted.

'What is the point then of raising the original credentials, if the word "conclude" did not mean that when you had signed it was ended?' the President asked.

Griffith settled the issue by pointing out that while the plenipotentiaries may have had the power to commit the Dáil to a treaty, this had not been done. Neither they nor the British signatories had bound their nations by their signatures. 'They had to go to their parliament,' he said, 'and we to ours.'

People had sensed the momentous implications of the credentials authorising the delegation to 'conclude' a Treaty, so Griffith's explanation was greeted with relieved applause by deputies. 'One felt that they were glad at being told so bluntly by the Chairman of the Delegation of plenipotentiaries that they had the fullest and most perfect freedom of action in the discussion over ratification,' a reporter noted. 'Eamon de Valera for the first time smiled — not a mocking or ironical smile but one that illuminated his grave and austere features.'[20]

The Dáil then quickly agreed to go into private session, during which the President again raised the issue of the powers of the delegation. Though some people were confused about those powers, de Valera left no doubt that the plenipotentiaries had the right to sign the agreement. 'Now I would like everybody clearly to understand', he emphasised, 'that the plentipotentiaries went over to negotiate a Treaty, that they could differ from the cabinet if they wanted to, and that in anything of consequence they could take their decision against the decision of the cabinet.' He actually stressed that same point in the Dáil at least four times during the debate.

The President's position, in short, was that the plenipotentiaries had the right to sign but should not have done so in view of Griffith's undertaking not to sign the draft treaty. Collins, who admitted Griffith had said he would not sign 'that document', contended that the undertaking had not been violated seeing that the proposals discussed at the cabinet meeting had been altered significantly in the final hours of the conference, with the result 'a different document was signed.' In this case, however, the new document should have been submitted to the cabinet in accordance with the instructions. There could be no doubt that Griffith had broken the undertaking involved in either his acceptance of the instructions or his declaration at the cabinet meeting that he would not sign the British draft terms being discussed at the time.

It was on the strength of Griffith's undertaking that the President had not gone over to London and rejected the British terms himself. According to his authorised biographers, de Valera privately felt he had been let down badly by the delegation. During December, for instance, he wrote to a friend in America:

> Not only did the delegation break their word, given a few days previously, that they would not sign any such document and disobey their instructions in not submitting the final text to Dublin, they were guilty further of an act of disloyalty to their President and to their colleagues in the Cabinet such as is probably without parrallel in history. They not merely signed the document but, in order to make the *fait accompli* doubly secure, they published it hours before the President or their colleagues saw it, and were already giving interviews in London proclaiming its merits and prejudicing the issue at the time it was being read in Dublin.[21]

The President was obviously annoyed that the plenipotentiaries had not taken their lead from him. 'I was captaining a team,' he told the private session on the first afternoon, 'and I felt that the team should have played with me to the last and I should have got the chance which I felt would put us over and we might have crossed the bar in my opinion at high tide. They rushed before the tide got to the top and almost foundered the ship.'

Resenting the remarks, Collins turned to those behind him and quietly derided de Valera as 'a captain who sent his crew to sea, and tried to direct operations from dry land.'[22]

During the afternoon Collins called several times for the release of the various documents relating to the latter stages of the negotiations so that deputies could determine for themselves the exact difference between the signed terms and what the dissident members of the cabinet had wanted. In particular, he argued that the counter proposals which were presented to the British on 4 December should be 'put side by side' with the Articles of Agreement. Otherwise people were likely to think that the cabinet members in Dublin had been standing for an isolated Republic whereas Collins believed that the difference between the Treaty and what de Valera, Brugha and Stack were prepared to accept was not worth fighting over.

On introducing his alternative treaty for the Dáil's consideration, de Valera made the startling admission that 'it is right to say that there will be a very little difference in practice between what I may call the proposals received and what you will have under what I propose. There is very little in practice but there is that big thing that you are consistent and that you recognise yourself as a separate independent State and you associate in an honourable manner with another group.' The President contended that if the Dáil stood by his counter proposals, the British would 'not go to war for the difference.' In short, he was arguing that the British would not fight over the difference while Collins was contending they would even though the difference was not worth fighting over.

'I felt the distance between the two was so small that the British would not wage war on account of it,' de Valera explained. 'You may say if it is so small why not take it. But I say, that small difference makes all the difference. This fight has lasted through the centuries and I would be willing to win that little sentimental thing that would satisfy the aspirations of the country.'

De Valera's alternative, which Collins dubbed 'Document No 2', incorporated External Association on the lines of the proposals put forward by the delegation during the final weeks of the London conference. There was no oath in the new proposals, but there was a stipulation that 'for the purposes of the Association, Ireland shall recognise His Britannic Majesty as head of the Association.' In defensive matters Britain would be afforded basically the same facilities as provided for in the Treaty, except that after five years the coastal defence of Ireland would be handed over 'to the Irish Government, unless some other arrangement for naval defence was agreed upon by both Governments.' The Treaty, on the other hand, merely provided that the two countries would reconsider the defence provisions in five years.

Document No 2 included partition clauses which were virtually identical with those in the Treaty, except there was a declaration to the effect that 'the right of any part of Ireland to be excluded from the supreme authority of the National Parliament and Government' was not being recognised. Nevertheless the alternative went on to include the Treaty's clauses relating to the partition question virtually *verbatim*. In other words, as de Valera himself explained, the alternative would not 'recognise the right of any part of Ireland to secede', but for the sake of internal peace and in order to divorce the Ulster question from the overall Anglo-Irish dispute, he was ready to accept the partition clauses of the Treaty, even though he found them objectionable from the standpoint that they provided 'an explicit recognition of the right on the part of Irishmen to secede from Ireland.'

'We will take the same things as agreed on there,' the President told the Dáil. 'Let us not start to fight with Ulster.'

Rejecting Document No 2, Collins said he would not try to explain his reasons until the public session reconvened. But he admitted he was glad that the proposals had been introduced because they clearly showed the division within the cabinet was only over a small difference. 'The issue,' he declared, 'has been cleared considerably by the document the President has put in.'

The alternative was basically in line with the proposals put forward by the delegation during the latter stages of the conference. 'We put this before the other side with all the energy we could,' Collins said. 'That is the reason that I wanted certain vital documents and these will show that the same proposals that the President has now drafted have been put already.'

As far as Collins was concerned it would be pointless trying to get the British to accept Document No 2. They had already rejected comparatively similar proposals on several occasions. He contended that they would not even give a hearing to any Irish delegation that tried to substitute the new document for the Treaty. 'You can go to the devil,' he predicted the British would say; 'you can't speak for anyone; you can't deliver the goods.'

In some respects Collins actually thought the Treaty was better than Document No 2. Describing the External Association clauses of the latter document as a dangerously loose paraphrase of the Treaty, he later complained that Ireland would be committed to an association so vague that Britain might be able to press for control in Irish affairs as a matter of common concern amongst the countries of the British Commonwealth. As Ireland would not have the same status as the Dominions, the latter would not have a vested interest in ensuring that the Dublin government would not be forced to make special concessions to Britain, seeing that such concessions would not establish a precedent for relations within the British Commonwealth as would be the case under the terms of the Treaty. Thus Collins complained that Document No 2 'had neither the honesty of complete isolation' nor the advantages of 'free partnership'. He admitted there were restrictions in both the Treaty and the President's alternative. *'But,'* he added, *'the Treaty will be operative, and the restrictions must gradually tend to disappear as we go on, more and more strongly solidifying and establishing ourselves as a free nation.'*[23] In short, the Treaty provided stepping stones to full freedom.

De Valera quickly realised, according to his authorised biographers, that his tactics in introducing Document No 2 had been ill-advised. On the one hand it tended to divide Republican elements — some of whom were unwilling to accept less than an isolated Republic. While on the other hand, the similarities between Document No 2 and the Treaty seemed to strengthen Collins' hand in arguing that the difference was not worth fighting over. De Valera therefore withdrew his proposal at the end of the private session.

When Collins entered the Dáil the following Monday, 19 December 1921, for the resumption of the public session, something was obviously wrong because he was not smiling as usual. Instead he had a sour expression and he slammed his attaché case down on the table in front of him as he took his seat. It soon became apparent what was irritating him.

On opening the session the Speaker announced that the President wished to inform the Dáil that Document No 2 was 'withdrawn and must be regarded as confidential until he brings his own proposal forward formally.' Griffith and Collins objected vociferously before the Speaker made it clear he was not ruling on the issue. Each individual deputy would be free to decide whether or not to comply with de Valera's request.

Griffith formally proposed that the Treaty be approved during a twenty minute speech in which he admitted the agreement was not 'the ideal thing' but was an honourable settlement that was good enough for 95 per cent of the Irish people. In an obvious attempt to use the popularity of Collins to enlist support for the agreement, he denounced the effort which was being made to depict Collins — whom he described as 'the man who won the war' — as having now 'compromised Ireland's right.' Intimating that the Republican position had really been abandoned before the delegation ever went to London, Griffith pointed out that not once during the correspondence which preceded the conference had the demand been made for recognition of the Irish Republic. 'If it had been made,' he said, 'we knew it would have been refused. We went there to see how to reconcile the two positions, and I hold we have done it.'

Seán Mac Eoin seconded the motion before de Valera appealed to the Dáil not to approve the Treaty. 'Standing with his body slightly bent,' the *Irish Times* reported, 'he poured withering scorn on this ignoble document. His voice rose to a high pitch of anger, falling at times to a deeper note of despair. It was a good speech in its way.'

'I am against this Treaty because it does not reconcile Irish national aspirations with association with the British Government,' de Valera declared. 'I am against this Treaty, not because I am a man of war, but a man of peace. I am against this Treaty because it will not end the centuries of conflict between the two nations of Great Britain and Ireland.'

The President, who never even alluded to the partition question, kept his remarks very general and avoided specific references to the Treaty, with the exception of condemning the oath. He contended that the Treaty was 'absolutely inconsistent with our position; it gives away Irish independence; it brings us into the British Empire; it acknowledges the head of the British Empire, not merely as the head of an association but as the direct monarch of Ireland, as the source of executive authority in Ireland.' If deputies accepted the agreement, he concluded, they would be 'presuming to set bounds on the onward march of a nation.'

Collins did not speak until immediately after a lunchtime break. As the Dáil re-assembled there was a great buzz of excitement and expectation. 'At the back of the hall visitors, clergymen and telegraph messengers crushed forward to hear,' according to the *Freeman's Journal*. 'A Japanese journalist was wedged in the crowd, and three coloured gentlemen from Trinidad — medical students — leant forward to view the scene' when Collins rose to continue the debate.

He was the focus of everyone's attention. 'His flashing eyes, firm jaw, and thick black hair, through which he ran his fingers from time to time, were all revealed under the dazzling light of the electroliers.'

'Mr Collins was passionate, forcible, and at times almost theatrical,' according to the *Irish Times*. Although he had a prepared speech before him, he rarely consulted it. Now and again he would rummage among his papers, feel his smooth chin, or toss his hair with one of his hands. At times he stood erect and at other times leaned forward. He spoke slowly until aroused, and then, vibrating with emotion, the words would come in a torrent.

Early in the address he complained that a deputy had suggested the delegation had broken down before the first bit of British bluff. 'I would remind the deputy who used that expression,' Collins said indignantly, 'that England put up a good bluff for the last five years here and I did not break down before that bluff.'

'That's the stuff,' someone shouted while the gathering applauded.

As one of the signatories, Collins said he was recommending the Treaty. 'I do not recommend it for more than it is,' he emphasised. 'Equally I do not recommend it for less than it is. In my opinion it gives us freedom, not the ultimate freedom that all nations desire and develop to, but the freedom to achieve it.' As a result of the guarantee of the constitutional status of Dominions like Canada and South Africa, he contended that those countries would be 'guarantors of our freedom, which makes us stronger than if we stood alone.' He admitted that allowing Britain to retain four ports was a 'departure from the Canadian status,' but he felt the Free State's association with the Dominions on an equal footing would ensure that Britain would not use the ports 'as a jumping off ground against us.' He also admitted the clauses relating to the Ulster question were 'not an ideal arrangement, but if our policy is, as has been stated, a policy of non-coercion, then let somebody else get a better way out of it.' He had planned to compare the Treaty with Document No 2 but explained that in deference to the President's request, he would not make use of his prepared arguments.

'Rejection of the Treaty means that your national policy is war,' Collins declared, 'I, as an individual, do not now, no more than ever shirk war. The Treaty was signed by me, not because they held up the alternative of immediate war. I signed it because I would not be one of those to commit the Irish people to war without the Irish people committing themselves.' This was a rather ironic statement coming from him in the light of his own role in deliberately trying to precipitate a state of general disorder back in 1919.

According to one seasoned parliamentarian, Collins' speech was 'worthy of a lawyer as well as a politician. It was big enough for a trained statesman. I was surprised by its precision and detail, and rhetoric,' Tim Healy wrote.[24] Interspersing the speech with some wry humour Collins observed that one deputy had complained the Free State could not enjoy the same freedom as Canada because that freedom was largely dependent on that country's distance from Britain. 'It seems to me,' Collins continued alluding to the same deputy, 'that he did not regard the delegation as being wholely without responsibility for the geographical propinquity of Great Britain to Ireland.' At another point Collins referred to those opposing the Treaty as a coalition of External Associationists and out-and-out isolated Republicans. There followed a moment of silence, and then a roar of laughter. 'I never saw Mr de Valera laugh more heartily or more unrestrainedly,' John Boyle of the *Irish Independent* reported. 'It was a wonderful relief — this glimmer of humour in a tense debate.'

The speech also contained what may have been a subtle effort to depict some of his leading opponents as something less that fully Irish. 'I am the representative of an Irish stock,' Collins said; 'I am the representative equally with any other member of the same stock of people who have suffered through the terror in the past. Our grandfathers have suffered from war, and our fathers or some of our ancestors have died of famine. I don't want a lecture from anybody as to what my principles are to be now. I am just a representative of plain Irish stock whose principles have been burned into them, and we don't want any assurance to the people of this country that we are going to betray them. We are one of themselves.' Few people could have failed to notice that some of the leaders on the other side of the floor — like the American-born de Valera with his Spanish father, or Childers and Brugha with their English backgrounds — were not able to boast of such a strong Irish ancestry.

It was a trying day for Collins, who afterwards explained to his fiancée that it was 'the worst day I ever spent in my life.' He wrote that 'the Treaty will almost certainly be beaten and then no one knows what will happen. The country is certainly quite clearly for it but that seems to be little good, as their voices are not heard.'[25]

According to Desmond Ryan, who witnessed the proceedings as a member of the staff of the *Freeman's Journal,* the debate developed into 'one long wrestle between ghosts and realities with all the stored up personal spleens of five years flaming through the rhetoric.'[26] Numerous speakers argued that various deceased heroes would never have accepted the Treaty.

'Out of the greatest respect for the dead,' Collins complained, 'we have refrained from reading letters from relatives of the dead. We have too much respect for the dead.' He thought that deputies should not presume to speak for those deceased, though he was understanding when Kathleen Clarke, the widow of one of the 1916 leaders, personally told him that evening she was going to vote against the Treaty, because she believed her late husband would have wished her to do so.

'I wouldn't want you to vote for it,' Collins told her. 'All I ask is that if it is passed, you give us the chance to work it.'[27]

With Christmas approaching and no likely end to the debate in sight, the Dáil decided to recess on 23

December until 3 January 1922. During that time the press, which was solidly behind the Treaty, encouraged local bodies to endorse the agreement, and more than twenty County Councils responded in a unanimous show of support. But the struggle for ratification was to become a long drawn-out affair.

6. As by Law Established

'I have strained every nerve to get support for the Treaty,' Collins told one of his sisters during the Christmas recess, 'but I'm hoping now we'll be defeated at the division.'

Puzzled, she asked him why.

'Either way,' he replied, 'there's going to be trouble.'[1] He felt it would be too divisive if the Dáil only approved the Treaty narrowly. Yet a narrow victory was the best he could expect. So when leaders of the Labour Party proposed a way to avoid a division in the Dáil, he supported their initiative.

In order to understand this initiative, however, it is first necessary to appreciate the exact nature of de Valera's objections to the Treaty. He had been concentrating his criticism on the obnoxious implications of the oath, which he characterised as an oath of allegiance to the British King. Yet the wording of the oath was in line with what he had proposed at the last cabinet meeting before the treaty was signed.

The President actually told the private session of the Dáil that he had suggested the Irish people could swear 'to keep faith with his Britannic Majesty.'[2] Moreover, on the eve of the Christmas recess he admitted to an American correspondent, Hayden Talbot of the Hearst newspaper chain, that his problem was not with swearing to be 'faithful to the King.'[3] He explained he did not find the word 'faithful' objectionable at all, because he did not look upon it as signifying the relationship between a slave and his master.

'I take it to mean that "faithful" is as regards a bargain made in the faithfulness of two equals who show it in keeping the bargain,' de Valera said. The real problem was the oath involved swearing 'allegiance to the constitution of the Irish Free State as by law established,' which, he argued, would amount to swearing allegiance to the Crown as the titular head of the Free State's constitution, seeing that the constitution itself would be enacted by the British parliament in the name of the King.

'The point is,' the President emphasised, 'that the oath contained in the Treaty actually and unequivocally binds the taker to "allegiance" to the English King, for under the terms of the Treaty the constitution of the Irish Free State "as by law established" is the King of England and nobody else.' For instance, the Provisional Government which would take over the administration of Ireland from the British would not be set up by the Dáil, but by the Southern Irish parliament established under the Partition Act passed at Westminster. Thus the Provisional Government would derive its authority from the British King, in whose name parliament had passed the Partition Act in the first place. In addition the Free State's constitution, which was to be drafted by the Provisional Government, would be enacted at Westminster, with the result that if the British had the acknowledged right to enact the Irish constitution in the name of the King, then it would automatically follow that they could amend that constitution if they wished. They would, in effect, be legally able to act in the King's name or interfere in Irish affairs at will.

Labour Party leaders suggested, however, that the Dáil should allow the Treaty to become operative by passing legislation to establish the Provisional Government as a committee of the Dáil itself. This would have the double advantage of affording the Irish people a practical opportunity of evaluating the freedom which could be secured under the Treaty, while at the same time providing a way of circumventing those aspects of the Treaty that de Valera found most objectionable.

From the practical standpoint it did not really matter to Collins whether Irish freedom was legally derived from the British or anyone else, so long as that freedom was real, but the President was disturbed by the implications of accepting an act of the British parliament as the source of Irish freedom, because it naturally followed that what the British had the authority to confer, they also had the authority to withdraw or modify. Hence de Valera's reluctance to swear allegiance to the Irish constitution 'as by law [i.e. British law] established.' But if the Dáil transferred the necessary authority to the Provisional Government and it then drew up an autochthonous constitution (that is a constitution which specifically derived its authority from the Irish people rather than from some outside source), its subsequent enactment by the British could be taken simply as a formal acknowledgment that the Irish people had an inherent right to govern themselves. The constitution could thus be seen as having been established by Dáil Éireann, acting on behalf of the Irish people, with the result that the obnoxious implications of the oath would be eliminated, seeing that those taking the oath would be entitled to feel they were swearing allegiance to the Free State's constitution as 'by [Irish] law established.'

Collins seemed amenable to the proposals when they were broached to him on 23 December 1921. 'I think they are the basis of something that can be hammered into an agreement,' he said.

Griffith, too, seemed hopeful on Christmas Day. The Labour leaders therefore had, what they described as, grounds 'to hope that a basis of agreement had been found', but 'this hope was shattered at the interview with Mr de Valera' two days later.[4]

Nevertheless Collins was not prepared to forget about the initiative so easily. When the Dáil reconvened on 3

January 1922 he suggested that it should accept the Treaty without a division and then authorise the setting up of the Provisional Government so that it could demonstrate practically the extent of the country's freedom. 'If necessary,' he said to those across the floor, 'you can fight the Provisional Government on the Republican question afterwards.'

'We will do that if you carry ratification, perhaps,' replied the President spurning the suggestion.

In an interview with the press that evening, Collins explained he was not asking his opponents to do anything dishonourable:

> They are not asked to abandon any principle; they may, if need be, act as guardians of the interests of the nation — act as guarantors of Irish requirements, and act as censors of the Government of the Irish Free State. The Government of the Irish Free State may have difficulties in carrying on and in fulfilling promises contained in the Treaty. If these promises are less in their working out than we who are standing for the Treaty declare, then there is a glorious opportunity for the present opponents of the Treaty to show their ability to guard the Irish nation and to act on its behalf. At the present moment we ask not to be hampered, and if we do not achieve what we desire and intend, we shall willingly make room for the others, and they will have no more loyal supporters than ourselves. This is the one way of restoring unity in the Dáil and to preserve [it] as a body truly representative of the Irish people.[5]

But de Valera had plans of his own. Next day he informed the Dáil that he was going to move a revised version of Document No 2 as an amendment. In response to objections that he had already agreed that no amendment to the Treaty could be considered until the Dáil first voted on the document, the President contended he was not actually moving an amendment to the Treaty itself but to the resolution calling for the Dáil's approval of the agreement. This raised the spectre of extending the already drawn-out debate, with each of the more than one hundred deputies being allowed to speak again — this time on the amendment. 'If that takes place,' one Cork deputy complained, 'we will go on for ever, or at least till the people come in and pull us out.'[6]

Collins argued that a vote should first be taken on the Treaty. He was supported by O'Higgins, but the President seemed determined to have his own way. In fact, he was so dogmatic that the political correspondent of the *Freeman's Journal* accused him of 'arrogating to himself the rights of an autocrat.'

'I am responsible for the proposals and the House will have to decide on them,' de Valera declared. 'I am going to choose my own procedure.'

The Dáil was staggered. Griffith rose and responded in a cold but intent manner: 'I submit it is not in the competence of the President to choose his own procedure. This is either a constitutional body or it is not. If it is an autocracy let you say so and we will leave it.'

'In answer to that I am going to propose an amendment in my own terms.' the President maintained defiantly. 'It is for the House to decide whether they will take it or not.' He seemed to want to 'hurl another few words across the floor, but the soothing hand of a supporter from the bench behind tapping him gently on the shoulder had a calming effect.'[7] The undignified spectacle was thus mercifully ended, and the Dáil recessed for the evening.

Immediately afterwards nine backbenchers representing various shades of opinion — among them Seán T. O'Kelly, Liam Mellows, Paddy Ruttledge, Eoin O'Duffy, and Michael Hayes — met at O'Kelly's home in an effort to find a formula that would prevent a complete split within Sinn Féin. With only Mellows dissenting, they came up with a proposal in line with the idea that opponents should abstain from voting against the Treaty and allow the Provisional Government to function drawing its powers from the Dáil, while de Valera would remain as President in order 'that every ounce can be got out of the Treaty.'[8]

Griffith and Collins accepted the plan that night, but O'Kelly was unable to contact de Valera. Unfortunately the atmosphere next morning was somewhat poisoned by a virulent attack on the President in an editorial in the *Freeman's Journal,* which charged that vanity had prompted him to make 'a criminal attempt to divide the nation' by pressing an alternative which was 'much worse' than the Treaty. The editorial went on to suggest that as he had 'not the instinct of the Irishman in his blood,' the Irish people should put 'their fate into the hands of their own countrymen,' like Griffith, Collins, and Mulcahy.

Whether or not Collins had wished to draw attention to the President's foreign background in his own Dáil speech a fortnight earlier, he quickly disassociated himself from the *Freeman's Journal* attack. He not only denounced it in the Dáil but also complained to the editor that he did not want his 'name to be associated with any personal attack on those who are opposed to me politically in the present crisis.'

De Valera remained deeply irritated by the attack however. Flatly rejecting the backbench initiative, he insisted that Document No 2 be accepted instead. Next morning, 6 January 1922, the Dáil went back into private session in order to consider the initiative, but the President was adamantly opposed.

'I am going to settle all this thing by resigning publicly at the public session,' he stated, banging the table in front of him. 'I am not going to connive at setting up in

Ireland another government for England.'

When the public session reconvened little over two hours later, the President announced his resignation in the course of a truly extraordinary speech. 'Even in his happiest moments Mr de Valera has scarcely surpassed himself in declaratory power,' observed one reporter, who noted that the remarkable address claimed the devoted attention of the whole Dáil.[9]

The President began slowly and deliberately, but his voice became charged with emotion as he defended his alternative. 'Now I have definitely a policy,' he explained, 'not some pet scheme of my own, but something that I know from four years' experience in my position — and I have been brought up amongst the Irish people. I was reared in a labourer's cottage here in Ireland.'

The Dáil applauded. This was obviously the President's answer to the snide questioning of his credentials as an Irishman by the *Freeman's Journal*.

'I have not lived solely amongst the intellectuals,' he continued. 'The first fifteen years of my life that formed my character were lived amongst the Irish people down in Limerick; therefore, I know what I am talking about; and whenever I wanted to know what the Irish people wanted I had only to examine my own heart and it told me straight off what the Irish people wanted.'

The President went on to announce his resignation, adding that the Dáil would have 'to decide before it does further work, who is to be the Chief Executive in this Nation.' He made it clear that he was going to stand for re-election. 'If you elect me and you do it by a majority,' he said, 'I will throw out that Treaty.'

It was then proposed and seconded that the standing orders should be suspended in order to discuss the crisis caused by the President's resignation. Collins was enraged.

'The other side may say what they like, and they may put in any motion they like, and they may take any action they like, but we must not criticise them. That is the position that we have been put into', he declared. 'We will have no Tammany Hall methods here. Whether you are for the Treaty or whether you are against it, fight without Tammany Hall methods. We will not have them.' He went on to complain that the backbench initiative to avoid a division had been frustrated by 'three or four bullies'.

De Valera objected to the use of the term, bullies, and the Speaker asked Collins to withdraw the remark. There followed an uneasy silence. Collins seemed to seek inspiration from the papers in front of him. Almost a minute passed before he responded.

'I can withdraw the term,' he emphasised slowly and deliberately, 'but the spoken word cannot be recalled. Is that right, sir?'

A showdown with the Speaker had been averted. Deputies laughed and the gathering applauded. But Brugha, who felt that he was one of those alluded to as a bully, was unhappy with the way that the remark had supposedly been withdrawn.

'In the ordinary way I would take exception and take offence at such a term being applied to me,' Brugha said, 'but the amount of offence that I would take at it would be measured by the respect or esteem that I had for the character of the person who made the charge. In this particular instance I take no offence whatever.' That slight was but a foretaste of the tirade which Brugha was to deliver the following day.

In the interim the President's rather obvious attempt to have the vote on the Treaty turned into a personal vote of confidence evoked so much criticism that he withdrew his resignation, but not before making some self-righteous remarks in the course of announcing his intention of actually retiring from politics. 'I am,' he said, 'sick and tired of politics — so sick that no matter what happens I would go back to private life. I have only seen politics within the last three weeks or a month. It is the first time I have seen them and I am sick to the heart of them.' He went on to depict himself as being straight and honest in the face of the twisted dishonesty of his opponents. 'It is because I am straight that I meet crookedness with straight dealing always,' he continued. 'Truth will always stand no matter from what direction it is attacked.'

'One of the most irritating features of Mr de Valera's behaviour at this time,' one Dáil deputy later wrote, 'was that, having used every device of a practical politician to gain his point, having shown himself relentless and unscrupulous in taking every advantage of generous opponents, he would adopt a tone of injured innocence when his shots failed, and assume the pose of a simple sensitive man, too guileless and gentle for this rough world of politics.'[10] Whether those opponents were indeed generous, as that deputy contended, may be open to question, but there can be no doubt that the President was being less than candid with his feigned innocence of the seamier side of politics. He had been up to his neck in such politics while in the United States. Indeed, he really refuted his own assertion of innocence later in the same speech by referring to his American experiences.

'I detest trickery,' de Valera said. 'What has sickened me most is that I got in this House the same sort of dealing that I was accustomed to over in America from other people of a similar kind.' It was particularly significant that he should compare his critics in the Dáil with his opponents in the United States, because there was really a remarkable similarity between the attitude he adopted towards the Treaty and his actions during the Republican Party's National Convention in Chicago in

June 1920. At that time he undermined a platform plank suggested by Cohalan — not for the reasons given publicly, but in order to demonstrate that he, not the judge, was the real spokesman for the Irish cause in America. Likewise during the Treaty debate, de Valera publicly emphasised that he was standing on a matter of principle by concentrating on the unacceptability of the oath. Yet he actually admitted during the private session that he might have accepted the oath earlier, but would have rejected it at the time of the signing because he believed that he could have done so 'with advantage to the nation'.[11] In short, his opposition to the oath was really more a question of tactics than principle. As a result it is difficult to avoid the conclusion that just as his attitude towards the Cohalan plank in Chicago had been prompted by his determination to show he was the real Irish spokesman in America, his attitude towards the Treaty was similarly influenced by his determination to show that he, not Collins, was the real Irish leader. Hence the President's resolute refusal to accept the Treaty, even under the terms urged upon him by Seán T. O'Kelly.

As the difference between the Treaty and Document No 2 was very small it was possibly inevitable that the debate should take on the aspects of a conflict of personalities with supporters of the Treaty massing behind Collins and opponents behind de Valera.

It was the personality of Collins, however, which loomed largest during the concluding speeches. Winding up the debate for the anti-Treaty side, for example, Brugha delivered a speech that quickly turned into a bitter personal attack on Collins, whom he described as 'merely a subordinate in the Department of Defence'. Persisting amid cries of 'Shame' and 'Get on with the Treaty', the Defence Minister complained that Collins himself had originated the story that there was a price on his head, and the press then built him into 'a romantic figure' and 'a mystical character' which he was not. But it was Griffith's reference to Collins as 'the man who won the war' that was most irritating to Brugha, who actually questioned whether Collins 'had ever fired a shot at any enemy of Ireland.'

For his part, Griffith made no apology for his earlier reference when he wound up the whole debate shortly afterwards:

> I said it, and I say it again; he was the man that made the situation; he was the man, and nobody knows better than I do how, during a year and a half he worked from six in the morning until two next morning. He was the man whose matchless energy, whose indomitable will carried Ireland through the terrible crisis; and though I have not now, and never had, an ambition about either political affairs or history, if my name is to go down in history I want it associated with the name of Michael Collins. Michael Collins was the man who fought the Black and Tan terror for twelve months, until England was forced to offer terms.

The Dáil erupted with a roar of approval and thunderous applause. It was without doubt the most emotional response of the whole debate. Deputies who had listened to Brugha's invective in embarrassed silence obviously jumped at the opportunity of disassociating themselves from those remarks.

Griffith's speech, which was described as 'by far the most statesmanlike utterance that has been made in the Dáil,' delivered some telling arguments in favour of the Treaty.[12] 'The principle that I have stood on all my life is the principle of Ireland for the Irish people. If I can get that with a Republic I will have a Republic; if I can get that with a monarchy I will have a monarchy. I will not sacrifice my country for a form of government,' he concluded. 'I say now to the people of Ireland that it is their right to see that this Treaty is carried into operation, when they get, for the first time in seven centuries, a chance to live their lives in their own country and take their place among the nations of Europe.'

As the proposer of the resolution calling for the Dáil's approval of the Treaty, Griffith was supposed to have the last word before the vote was taken, but de Valera again violated the procedure.

'Before you take a vote,' he said, 'I want to enter my last protest — that document will rise in judgment against the men who say there is only a shadow of difference.' He was apparently calling on deputies to reject the Treaty in favour of his Document No 2.

'Let the Irish nation judge us now and for future years,' cried Collins.

The clerk of the Dáil then began calling the role in order of the constituencies. Armagh came first, so it fell to Collins to cast the initial vote. With a faint smile, he rose, paused momentarily, and answered slowly, '*Is toil.*' The clerk continued through the other names, with deputies voting either, '*Is toil,*' or '*Ní toil.*'

When the names of deputies from Cork were reached, Collins was again called upon, but he declined to vote on the grounds that he had voted already. Likewise, when de Valera was called for his second constituency, he declined to vote by shaking his head slowly and smiling across at Collins. But Griffith protested at the disenfranchisement of his second constituency.

It took about ten minutes to complete the voting, and another couple of minutes followed before the announcement was made that the Treaty had been approved by 64 votes to 57. There was no real demonstration within the hall, but when the news filtered outside there was a wave of enthusiastic cheering in the street, where a crowd of several hundreds had gathered. The cheering lasted for some minutes and seemed to give life to those inside the chamber.

'It will, of course, be my duty to resign my office as Chief Executive,' de Valera said. 'I do not know that I should do it just now.'

'No,' cried Collins.

'There is one thing I want to say — I want it to go to the country and to the world, and it is this: the Irish people established a Republic. This is simply approval of a certain resolution. The Republic can only be disestablished by the Irish people. Therefore, until such time as the Irish people in a regular manner disestablish it, this Republic goes on.'

Collins called for a committee to be drawn from both sides of the Dáil to preserve order. Some people thought that de Valera was about to respond favourably. But Mary MacSwiney, 'who seemed obsessed by a consuming rage,' denounced what the Dáil had done 'as the greatest act of betrayal that Ireland ever endured.'

'I tell you here,' she said, 'there can be no union between the representatives of the Irish Republic and the so-called Free State.'

Collins repeated his appeal for 'some kind of understanding' between the two factions 'to preserve the present order in the country.' And de Valera again rose. 'I would like my last word here to be this,' he said: 'we have had a glorious record of four years, it has been four years of magnificent discipline in our nation. The world is looking at us now—'

At that point he broke down, buried his head in his hands, and collapsed sobbing into his chair. It was an intensely emotional scene. Women were weeping openly, and Harry Boland was seen with tears running down his cheeks, while other men were visibly trying to restrain their tears.

'So far as I am concerned,' Brugha declared amid the

scene, 'I will see at any rate, that discipline is kept in the army.'

'Do you know, in spite of all,' Collins said afterwards, 'I can't help feeling a regard for Cathal.'[13]

This admiration for Brugha was indicative of a character trait that was to cause endless difficulties for Collins in the following months. Reluctant to break with many of his former friends, even though their attitude left him with no alternative but to abandon the Treaty or lose their friendship, he displayed a real weakness in his leadership by vacillating in a vain attempt to reconcile their irreconcilable views. He was particularly disturbed by the growing rift between himself and such people as Harry Boland and de Valera.

> 'I am more sorry than you are that the President and Harry are on the other side from myself,' he wrote to a friend of Boland in January 1922. 'I believe they have missed the tide, for, were it not for taking the bold course I am certain this country would have been split by contending factions, whether we liked it or not. If there be but good will on all sides I am convinced we may still bring the whole thing to final success. In any case, we are going forward, the English are evacuating this country, and surely no one will claim that we can possible be worse off when that evacuation is complete.'[14]

Although de Valera had adopted the democratic line of insisting in the Dáil that only the Irish people could ratify the Treaty, his public pronouncements soon gave rise to grave doubts about his commitment to democracy. Having resigned as President and narrowly failing to win re-election, he walked out of the Dáil in protest against Griffith's election, and he refused to have any part in the formation of the Provisional Government, which Collins was elected to head. The former President proceeded to demonstrate a distinct unwillingness even to allow the issue of the Treaty to be put to the people.

'De Valera at first insisted that the Treaty would never be accepted by the people,' Collins recalled. 'He declared that "the terms of this Agreement are in violent conflict with the wishes of the majority of this nation." But little by little he began to realise that this was not the case. Whereupon he sponsored the remarkable policy of saving the people from themselves by preventing their expressing their will!'[15]

During March 1922 the former President toured the country warning that if the Treaty were ratified, the Volunteers of the future would have to resort to civil strife in order to complete the work of the past five years. 'They would,' he said, 'have to wade through Irish blood, through the blood of the soldiers of the Irish Government, and through, perhaps, the blood of some of the members of the Government in order to get Irish freedom.'[16]

Though de Valera quickly explained that his remarks were intended merely as a realistic assessment of the likely outcome, rather than threatening civil war in the event that the Treaty was accepted by the electorate, some people felt that the effect of the speech was the same as if he had intended it as a threat. Collins was so critical that he actually contributed to the growing recrimination himself.

'Whatever Mr de Valera's meaning, the effect of his language is mischievous', Collins declared at a public meeting in Waterford. 'Our opponents are keeping passions alive, directing them from their legitimate use against the enemy who was standing in the way of our freedom — directing them now that the enemy has gone, for illegitimate use against the people of their own nation to deprive them of that freedom. And I say, deliberately, that in so doing Mr de Valera and his followers are proving themselves to be the greatest enemies that Ireland has ever had.'[17]

When anti-Treaty elements of the IRA renounced their pro-Treaty leadership, repudiated their allegiance to the Dáil, intimated their readiness to set up a military dictatorship, and revealed their intention not to allow a popular vote to be taken on the Treaty until Britain withdrew her threat of war, de Valera was — in his own words — 'so foolish as to defend their actions even to a straining of my own views.'[18] He stood by in apparent acquiescence as those anti-Treaty members of the IRA seized prominent Dublin buildings, including the Four Courts, where they set up their headquarters in the early hours of Good Friday, 14 April 1922.

Representatives of the Labour Party immediately called on de Valera to use his influence 'with a view to averting the impending calamity of civil war.'[19] But they found him unsympathetic when they argued that, as the Treaty had been accepted by the Dáil, it was his duty to observe the decision of the majority until reversed. His only response was to stress about a dozen times that the majority had 'no right to do wrong'.

Years later de Valera explained his remark. 'If you got a unanimous vote of the people telling you to go and shoot your neighbour, you would be quite in the wrong in carrying out that majority will,' he said. 'Therefore the majority rule does not give to anybody the right to do anything wrong, and I stand by the statement that a majority does not give a right to do wrong. What was wrong in that statement? It was simply the truth. To quote Kipling, the truth I had spoken was "twisted by knaves to make a trap for fools".'[20]

Although not responsible for the duplicity of knaves or the stupidity of fools, de Valera certainly gave knaves and fools ample opportunities to misrepresent him. Only hours after the seizing of the Four Courts, for example, he issued an Easter proclamation that ended with an appeal which could only be classed as provocative in the light of recent events. 'Young men and young women of Ireland, the goal is at last in sight,' he concluded. 'Steady; all together; forward. Ireland is yours for the taking. Take it.'[21]

Even if he had never meant to encourage civil strife, he certainly did very little to discourage it. He remained silent, for instance, while some of those closest to him, like Brugha or Harry Boland, made no secret of the fact that they were threatening civil war. Boland, who was acting as de Valera's secretary, wrote at the time that 'civil war is certain unless Collins and Company see the error of their way and come to terms with their late colleagues.'[22]

The Catholic archbishop of Dublin tried to head off the impending disaster by getting the two sides together for a conference in late April, but it proved impossible to make progress in the face of the growing personal bitterness. At one point in the conference, for example, Brugha referred to Griffith and Collins as British agents. When they jumped to their feet in protest, the archbishop requested that the remark be withdrawn. Brugha agreed but added that he regarded any people who did the work of the British government as agents, which only added to the tension.

Collins was furious. With both hands firmly planted on the table, he leaned forward towards Brugha. 'I suppose,' he said, 'we are two of the Ministers whose blood is to be waded through!'

'Yes,' replied Brugha in his quiet, distinct way, 'you are two.'[23]

De Valera made no secret of his sympathy with those who were refusing to allow elections to be held, even though this was clearly in violation of an agreement he had made with Griffith and Collins at the Sinn Féin Árd Fheis in February. Then, they had agreed to postpone elections for three months and to publish the Free State constitution beforehand so that the people would have a better idea of the implications of the Treaty. But within a month de Valera was looking for a further delay in order to update the electoral register.

Griffith refused to accept a further delay. He and Collins were anxious that the people should be allowed to endorse the Treaty as soon as possible, but they needed co-operation if massive intimidation was to be avoided. They therefore offered to arrange a referendum of all adults, whether on the register or not. This would be accomplished by having the people congregate at the same time in designated localities throughout the country. They would then signify their preferences openly by going to appropriate areas or passing through specific barriers designated for supporters or opponents of the Treaty. Although de Valera rejected the use of such 'stone age machinery', his prime concern was clearly not inspired by democratic principles, seeing that he publicly justified his refusal to co-operate on the grounds that there were 'rights which a minority may justly uphold, even by arms, against a majority.'[24]

'We all believe in democracy,' the former President told an American correspondent a fortnight later, 'but we do not forget its well-known weaknesses. As a safeguard against their consequences the most democratic countries have devised checks and brakes against sudden changes of opinion and hasty, ill-considered decisions.' In the United States, for example, a treaty needed the approval of a two-thirds majority of the Senate. Since the Irish system had 'not yet had an opportunity of devising constitutional checks and brakes,' de Valera implied that the anti-Treaty elements of the IRA were justified both in refusing to accept the decision of the majority of the Dáil and in taking the initiative in trying to prevent an election in which the Treaty would be the issue. 'The Army sees in itself the only brake at the present time,' he said, 'and is using its strength as such.'[25]

Although Collins was never known for his patience, he did reveal an extraordinary toleration during those weeks in which de Valera and others were supposedly saving the people from themselves. Even Griffith, renowned for his pacifism, wanted to clear out the Four Courts, where the garrison had assumed the right to rob banks, commandeer vehicles, and appropriate supplies without paying for them. On occasions Collins' patience seemed exhausted, but each time he would temporise and try to find some new avenue to avoid that final break with those militants with whom he had worked so efficiently during the Black and Tan struggle.

In trying to bridge the gap with his opponents he tended to over-state his own case, which led to some questioning of his veracity. He told Sean T. O'Kelly, for instance, that 'the English are ready to give us all that is contained in Document No 2.'[26]

'Why the duce then don't you press them to do so?' O'Kelly asked.

Collins had indeed been convinced during the London conference that the British were prepared to concede the *de facto* position that Document No 2 subsequently sought. Hence he planned to have a constitution drafted that would formalise the real position governing relations between Britain and the Dominions, rather than the existing legal position. In effect, he would have a constitution drafted which would be Republican in all but name. There would be an autochthonous clause stating that the legislative, executive, and judicial authority of the Free State was being derived solely from the Irish people, who would have the right to change the constitution by referendum called either by the legislature or by public petition.

There would also be a provision to the effect that only the Free State Parliament could declare war on behalf of the country, which would thus enshrine in the constitution the right to remain neutral while Britain was at war — the prized right which de Valera had declared would make 'a clean sweep' of the whole defence question during the Treaty negotiations.[27] Collins also thought that he would be able to have the Treaty-oath excluded from the constitution. His legal advisers had told him that even though the Treaty had stipulated 'the oath to be taken by members of the Parliament of the Irish Free State' would be as quoted, it did not specifically state that the oath had to be taken. In other words, members of the parliament need not take any oath, but if there were one, it would be as prescribed in the Treaty. In pursuing that line Collins was certainly stretching things, but he nevertheless indicated not only his willingness to press the matter but also his confidence of doing so successfully. 'The only explanation for Collins' optimism,' according to Professor Joseph M. Curran, 'is that his legal advisers were breathing the rarefied air of constitutional theory, untainted by political realities, while he himself ignored those realities because of his desperate desire for a Republican constitution.'[28]

In the last analysis, however, Collins was prepared to push the case only to a point short of actually breaking with the British. He was not willing to renew hostilities over the symbolism that constituted the essential difference between the Treaty and Document No 2. 'I certainly would not ask any Irishman,' Collins wrote, 'to risk his own life or to take the life of a fellow Irishman for the difference — the difference which was described by Mr de Valera himself as "only a shadow".'[29]

Even though Collins had indicated as early as February 1922 that he was prepared to insist there should be no oath, the gulf between himself and de

Valera had continued to widen during the following weeks. There was therefore genuine surprise on 20 May when the two of them concluded an electoral pact in accordance with which the two sections of Sinn Féin would put forward a united panel of candidates in proportion to their existing strength in the Dáil. Then if the party won a majority of seats, the portfolios within the new government would be allocated on a five to four ratio in favour of the pro-Treaty segment. As a result the Treaty would not really be an issue among Sinn Féin candidates, though other parties were supposedly free to contest the election on any platform they wished.

Griffith reluctantly agreed to the pact while the British were highly suspicious, but Collins explained it was the only way to ensure that the general election could be held. If nothing else, he felt that once the new constitution was published before the people went to the polls it would undermine the existing argument that the Dáil had been elected to uphold the Irish Republic with the result that it did not have the authority to implement the Treaty.

Collins tried to use the election deadline to rush the British into approving the constitution drafted by the Provisional Government. Although they accepted the autochthonous, referenda, and neutrality provisions, the British balked at the exclusion of the oath. And in the face of their insistence Collins eventually relented and agreed to include the oath in the constitution, as well as some of the more obnoxious aspects of monarchial symbolism, such as having the Free State parliament convene and having its executive function in the name of the King. In addition, the Treaty was scheduled to the constitution with the stipulation that in any matter in which there was a conflict between the two, the former would take precedence. While the 'archaic symbols' of the British Commonwealth had to be included in the Free State's constitution, one eminent legal authority noted that 'their meaninglessness for Ireland was writ large on every page. The monarchial forms paled into insignificance in the light of the formal enunciation and consistent application of the principle of the sovereignty of the people as the fundamental and exclusive source of all political authority.'[30]

The text of the constitution was only released on the eve of the election, so the Irish people did not have a chance to see the document until it was published in the daily press on polling day, which, of course, effectively denied critics that chance of explaining the document before voting, which was an essential aspect of the Árd Fheis agreement. But de Valera and his colleagues had already shown little respect for that agreement by their earlier threats to prevent the election. In fact, it would have been impossible to have balloting in anything like a normal atmosphere had Collins not agreed to the pact with de Valera. Under the circumstances therefore it should hardly have been too surprising that Collins showed little respect for the spirit of that pact. Two days before the election he told a public meeting in Cork that he was 'not hampered now by being on a platform where there are coalitionists and I can make a straight appeal to you, to the citizens of Cork, to vote for the candidates you think best of, whom the electors of Cork think will carry on best in the future the work that they want carried on.'

Even though Sinn Féin had deliberately avoided making the Treaty an election issue, there could be no doubt that the people favoured the Treaty. Of the party's 65 pro-Treaty candidates, for example, 58 were elected, while only 35 of the anti-Treaty people were successful. But even those figures exaggerated the anti-Treaty support, seeing that 16 of the anti-Treaty candidates were returned without opposition — in a number of cases after intimidation had been used to get other candidates to withdraw. Where the seats were fully contested, 41 of 48 pro-Treaty candidates won, which was over 89 percent, while only 19 of the 41 anti-Treaty candidates were elected, which amounted to barely 46 per cent. The popular vote painted an even bleaker picture for the anti-Treaty people, who received less than 22 per cent of the first preference votes cast. As a result there could be no doubt that the Irish electorate favoured accepting the Treaty — even de Valera accepted that the verdict had 'undoubtedly' gone against the Republicans.[31] It was obvious that the people were ready to accept the Treaty, at least as a stepping stone to full freedom.

In time it would become apparent that Collins was right about the controversial aspects of the Treaty. It did provide the freedom for the Free State to achieve complete political independence. During the 1930s de Valera and his Fianna Fáil government disestablished all aspects of the Treaty which he had criticised in December 1921. He even managed to acquire for himself much of the credit for securing the country's independence, seeing that the successors of Collins and Griffith, blinded by bitterness over the role that he played in fomenting the Treaty split, opposed most of his efforts to dismantle the Treaty. Yet in the last analysis de Valera and his colleagues really demonstrated that the freedom to achieve the desired freedom already existed. In effect, de Valera proved that Collins had been right.[32]

Of course, Collins miscalculated in the case of the Treaty's clauses relating to Northern Ireland. He had been convinced that if the Six Counties did not agree to unity, the area would be re-partitioned by the Boundary Commission so that what would remain of Northern Ireland would become an unviable ecomomic entity. On 28

February 1922 he wrote for instance, that:

> forces of persuasion and pressure are embodied in the Treaty. . . to induce North East Ulster to join in a United Ireland. If she joins in, the six counties will certainly have a generous measure of local autonomy. If she stays out, the decision of the Boundary Commission arranged for in Clause 12 would be certain to deprive her of Fermanagh and Tyrone. Shorn of those counties she would shrink into insignificance. The burdens of financial restrictions of the Partition Act will remain on North East Ulster, if she decides to stay outside of Ireland. No lightening of these burdens can be effected by the English Parliament without the consent of Ireland. Thus union is certain.[33]

Why was Collins so sure that the Boundary Commission would transfer large areas to the Free State? Some people contended that he had been given secret assurance by the British, but no convincing evidence of any such guarantee has ever been produced.* Yet on the morning before the Treaty was signed, Lloyd George did admit that if Collins' assessment of the Ulster situation was correct, then the Boundary Commission would hand over Fermanagh and Tyrone, together with Derry City and the southern parts of Armagh and Down. But that was not a commitment; it was merely an assessment which was contingent on the accuracy of Collins' judgement.

Nevertheless Lloyd George did publicly give grounds for believing that Fermanagh and Tyrone would be transferred. During the debate on the Treaty in the House of Commons he explained that those areas could remain part of Northern Ireland only by coercion. 'Although I am against the coercion of Ulster,' he continued, 'I do not believe in Ulster coercing other units.'

---

* See Appendix.

From this speech there could be little doubt that he expected the two counties would be given to the Free State, though he did tell his cabinet privately that the Boundary Commission could 'possibly give Ulster more than she would lose'.[34]

Collins may have believed that, as his influence was vital to securing Irish acceptance of the Treaty, the British would be afraid not to transfer the nationalist areas to the Free State for fear of antagonising him. They knew that he was convinced that those areas should be transferred, so they would run the risk of him denouncing the Treaty and declaring a Republic, if the areas were not handed over. Austen Chamberlain actually told the House of Commons that Britain would have to resume the war 'and fight for no great issue of national honour, for no great issue of imperial strength, but in order that you may preserve within the boundary of the Northern government populations, the majority of which desire to leave their sway.'

Since even the Ulster Unionists believed it was intended that the Boundary Commission would transfer large areas, public opinion would in all likelihood conclude that the British had violated the Treaty if the nationalist areas were not transferred. If, under those circumstances, Collins declared a Republic and Britain retaliated by declaring war, the British would have to fight without the public support for which they had negotiated in the first place. Consequently there were ample grounds for believing that the Boundary Commission would recommend a significant re-partitioning of Ulster.

Collins was therefore hopeful that the Belfast regime would agree to Irish unity provided that there were safeguards for the rights of Protestants and local autonomy for the area in which that minority actually constituted a majority, but he realised that the unrest in the Twenty-six Counties was seriously damaging those prospects.

'The immediate and continuing need,' he wrote shortly before his death, 'is for unity at home and real freedom — from our own outlaws and bandits as much from Black and Tans. We must have a period of peaceful development so that our civilisation may be a credit to us, and so that it will attract and be imitated instead of being a disgrace and humiliation to us.'[35]

By the time the Boundary Commission eventually met in 1924 Collins was dead and the Free State had been discredited by a savage and idiotic civil war, with the result that the Dublin government was in no position to react forcefully when the commission decided to recommend only the transfer of insignificant areas. Had the contiguous nationalist areas of Northern Ireland been transferred to the Free State as Collins had confidently expected, events in the North might well have taken a different course seeing that much of the bitterness over the years has been perpetuated by Protestant suppression of the Catholic minority lest that minority should gain control and unite with the rest of the island. But those tensions might not have existed had the Six Counties been re-partitioned, because the Catholic minority would then have been too small to pose a serious threat to Protestant power. Harmony might then have developed in much the same way as in the rest of the island.

Whether Michael Collins would ever have been able to make progress towards the ending of partition must remain a matter for conjecture. Yet there can be no doubt that he was right about the most controversial matters in the Treaty. He realised on signing the agreement that he was risking his life; but he signed because he believed it was in the interest of the Irish people. Had he been wrong, his courage and self-sacrifice would still demand the utmost respect. But he was not wrong. The Treaty was a 'real step' towards Irish freedom.

Appendix

Each night during the Treaty debate Collins used to meet some IRB colleagues, among them Ó Muirthile, McGrath, and P. S. O'Hegarty. On one evening O'Hegarty remarked with suprise about how little the partition question had figured in the debate.

'It's an astonishing thing to me,' he said, 'that in the attack on the Treaty practically nothing is said about partition, which is the one real blot on it.'

'Oh, but that is provided for,' replied Ó Muirthile. 'Didn't you know?'

'I did not, and how is it provided for? Ulster will opt out.'

'Before they signed,' Ó Muirthile explained, 'Griffith and Collins got a personal undertaking from Smith [Birkenhead] and Churchill that if Ulster opted out they would get only four counties and that *they* would make a four-county government impossible.'

O'Hegarty looked over at Collins, who grinned and confirmed the story. 'That's right,' he said.[1]

While such a promise may have been made, Collins should have secured it in writing. Seán Mac Eoin later contended that such a commitment was obtained in writing. He explained that before the Treaty was signed it had been agreed that a plebiscite would be held in electoral areas on the border. The plebiscite was supposed to be held by *arrondissements*. 'The draftsman or the typist left out these *operative words,'* according to Mac Eoin. 'When Collins realised this he complained that his legal staff "did not serve him well".' He got on to the British, but they explained that it was too late to alter the agreement. 'Collins then got a letter from Lord Birkenhead telling him,' Mac Eoin continued, 'that if the Six Counties opted out of the all Ireland parliament, the British Government agreed that instead of one representative on the Boundary Commission they would accept Collins' nomination of their man and this gave the Free State two members instead of one. This would rectify the situation in Ireland's favour. Collins gave me that letter to read.' After Collins' death, however, no trace could be found of the letter.[2]

Ernest Blythe, the last surviving member of the Free State delegation that negotiated the agreement doing away with the Boundary Commission, adamantly rejected the idea that Collins or Griffith had been given any kind of assurance. 'I was present at a good many cabinet meetings with both in the early months of 1922,' he recalled, 'and I never heard either of them say anything of the kind. Of course both believed in making our maximum claim and both hoped for the best, and people may have confused what they said we should claim with what they believed we might get.'[3]

On one occasion when Kevin O'Higgins asked Lloyd George about the territory which the Free State was likely to get, Blythe recorded that the reply was completely non-committal. 'Who am I to say what a judicial commission will decide?' responded the Prime Minister.[4]

O'Hegarty was 'unlikely to be given anything but the stock answer' by Collins, according to Blythe, who dismissed Mac Eoin's story as 'more or less absurd'. Blythe wrote:

> The idea that the intended words were left out of the Treaty without the Irish signatories realising it, is too like a schoolboy's yarn. If you can believe that it was arranged that the Free State would have two out of three members on the Boundary Commission you could believe that Hitler started the Second World War solely because the last held Consistory at the Vatican did not elect him Pope.

If you knew Seán Mac Eoin even fairly well you would know that while reliable when telling about his own exploits he inclines to give play to his imagination and his sense of the dramatic when he is talking about other people, and wants to make his story sound a little sensational. I venture to say that no one knowing him even fairly well would attach any importance to testimony from him which, on a matter not directly concerning himself, was intrinsically unlikely.

Birkenhead may, like all men, have been foolish in some respects, but he certainly was not enough of a blithering idiot to write a letter of the kind suggested. Whatever he may have done during negotiations by way of inuendo or private hint to suggest vaguely the possibility of substantial transfers to the Free State we can be sure that he did not speak as suggested by Mac Eoin.

I regard it as certain that he, as a politician of proven ability to survive, never definitely committed himself to the view that the Free State would get two counties or the equivalent of two counties from the North.[5]

There is no hint of any such letter from Birkenhead among Collins' papers, and his nephew who has those papers explained that he never before even heard about such a document. Lord Birkenhead's son was also surprised by the story as there was no copy of the letter among his father's papers. Unfortunately Collins did not make any entry in his diary for the two weeks following the Treaty, or if he did it was among papers which mysteriously vanished. It was not until 1963, for instance, that the Collins family actually got their hands on the diary covering the last eight days of his life. The earlier diaries have since been lost — having been lent to a journalist who did not return them.

Of course, if Collins had been given the letter, as suggested by Mac Eoin, it would have been highly confidential, and he was not likely to have shown it to many people. But Mac Eoin did claim to have read it and that was a matter in which he was personally involved, even if he did give play to his imagination in regard to the matters leading up to the letter.

Strange as it may seem, some operative words were indeed left out of the Treaty, and these were included the following day when the Irish delegation found that the word 'treaty' had never been mentioned. The document had just been entitled 'Proposed Articles of Agreement' and upon signing, the word 'Proposed' was blacked out. Childers telephoned Jones and got the first page re-typed to read, 'Articles of Agreement for a Treaty between Great Britain and Ireland, December 6, 1921.'[6]

So Mac Eoin's story about the omission of important words from the Treaty was not as fantastic as Blythe had thought. What was more, Collins did pay a highly secret visit to Lord Birkenhead during the debate in the Dáil. Shortly before Christmas, for instance, Birkenhead told a friend that he had had a secret midnight visit from Collins a few nights earlier.[7] He did not say what they discussed but it is just possible that if the letter mentioned by Mac Eoin ever existed, it could have been written that night.

But when Collins later claimed publicly that substantial areas of Northern Ireland would be transferred by the Boundary Commission, Birkenhead privately refuted the suggestion. 'The real truth,' he wrote, 'is that Collins, very likely pressed by his own people and anxious to appraise at their highest value the benefits which he had brought to them in a moment of excitement, committed himself unguardedly to this doctrine, and that it has no foundation whatever except in his overheated imagination.'[8] Those did not seem like the sentiments of a man who had given a secret assurance that the predictions of Collins would come to fruition. The story is repeated here for what it is worth.

NOTES

Chapter 1

1. Frank O'Connor, *The Big Fellow*, 134.
2. Desmond Ryan, *Remembering Sion,* 233.
3. Collins to Austin Stack, 10/2/19, Stack Papers.
4. Desmond Ryan, *Unique Dictator,* 100.
5. Darrell Figgis, *Recollections of the Irish War,* 241-3.
6. Earl of Longford and Thomas O'Nelll, *Eamon de Valera,* 90.
7. de Valera to Griffith, 17/2/20 and 6/3/20, DE 2/245, SPO.
8. de Valera to Griffith, 6/3/20.
9. Patrick McCartan, *With de Valera in America,* 153.
10. *Philadelphia Public Ledger,* 26/8/20.
11. *Gaelic American,* 4, 11/9/20.
12. Collins to Devoy, 30/9/20, *Irish Press* (Philadelphia), 6/11/20.
13. *Gaelic American,* 9/10/20.
14. Griffith to Moylett, 16/11/20, DE 2/251, SPO.
15. F.P. Crozier, *Ireland for Ever,* 218-9.
16. Robert Kee, *Ireland: A History,* 188.
17. Desmond Fitzgerald to D. O'Hegarty, 29/11/20, DE 2/234, SPO.
18. Collins to Art O'Brien, 6/12/20, DE 2/234, SPO.
19. Collins to O'Keeffe, 6/12/20.
20. O'Brien to Collins, 9/12/20, DE 2/234, SPO.
21. H.C. *Debates,* 135:260-7.
22. Griffith to Collins, 13/12/20, Piaras Beaslaí, *Michael Collins,* 2:123-5.
23. Collins to Griffith, 14/12/20, *Ibid.*, 2:126.
24. Collins to O'Brien, 15/12/20, DE 2/234, SPO.
25. Beaslaí, 2:136.
26. Thomas Jones, *Whitehall Diary,* 3:47.
27. de Valera to Collins, 18/1/21, DE 2/448.
28. Frank O'Connor, 20.
29. Robert Brennan, *Allegiance,* 153.
30. Ryan, *Remembering Sion,* 229, 231-2.
31. Frank Pakenham, *Peace by Ordeal,* 81; Padraig Colum, *Arthur Griffith,* 264.
32. Pakenham, *Ibid.*
33. Tom Barry, *Guerrilla Days in Ireland,* 164.
34. Ormonde Winter, *Winter's Tale,* 345.
35. Beaslaí, 2:173.
36. Collins to O'Hegarty, 9/12/20, DE 2/234, SPO.
37. O'Hegarty to Fitzgerald, 9/12/20, *Ibid.*
38. Jones, 3:48-9.
39. *Gaelic American,* 19/2/21.
40. de Valera to Harry Boland, quoted in Boland to James O'Mara,

29/3/21, O'Mara Papers, MS 21,549, NLI.
41. Ernie O'Malley, *Army Without Banners,* 294.
42. Longford and O'Neill, 148.
43. Colum, 264.
44. Leon Ó Broin, *Michael Collins,* 76.
45. Collins to Griffith, 26/1/21, Beaslaí, 2:152.
46. *Freeman's Journal,* 22/4/21.
47. Jones, 3:55.
48. *Ibid.,* 60.
49. Lord Riddell, *Intimate Diary of the Peace Conference and After,* 228.
50. Jones, 3:68-70.

Chapter 2

1. Collins to de Valera, 16/6/21, DE 2/244, SPO.
2. *Daily News,* 1/6/21.
3. Collins to de Valera, 3/6/21, DE 2/526, SPO.
4. Winston S. Churchill, *The Aftermath,* 290.
5. For de Valera's conversation with Smuts see, Smuts, 'de Valera's position — Dublin Meeting,' 5/7/21, *Smuts Papers,* 5:94-5; Smut's account to British cabinet, 6/7/21, Jones, 3:82-5; memo of conversation between Smuts and King George V, 7/7/21, *Smuts Papers,* 5:95-8.
6. Longford and O'Neill, 132.
7. de Valera to Collins, 15/7/21, DE 2/262, SPO.
8. de Valera to Collins, 19/7/21.
9. de Valera to Lloyd George, 19/7/21.
10. de Valera to McGarrity, 27/12/21, J. McGarrity Papers, MS. 17,440, NLI.
11. Lloyd George to King George V, 21/7/21, Nicolson, 357.
12. *Ibid.*
13. Stack, 'Own Account of Negotiations,' MS. 6 Stack Papers.
14. Collins to de Valera, 20/7/21, DE 2/262, SPO.
15. Neville Macready, *Annals of an Active Life,* 585.
16. *Irish Times,* 8/8/21.
17. *Freeman's Journal,* 9/8/21.
18. Beaslaí, 2:280.
19. de Valera to Devoy, 7/2/18, John Devoy Papers, MS. 18003, NLI.
20. Dáil, *Private Sessions,* 29.
21. Dáil, Official Report: For period 16th August, 1921 to 26 August, 1921, 9.
22. Dáil, *Debate on the Treaty,* 25.
23. Dáil, *Private Sessions,* 57.
24. *Ibid.,* 58-9.
25. Stack, 9.
26. Collins interview with Hayden Talbot, 2/8/22, MS, (Private Source); see also Talbot, *Michael Collins' Own Story,* 144-51.

27. *Ibid.*
28. de Valera to McGarrity, 27/12/21.
29. *Ibid.*
30. *Ibid.*
31. *Ibid.*
32. Dáil, *Private Sessions,* 96.
33. Beaslaí, 2:275.
34. Dáil, *Private Sessions,* 96.
35. Beaslaí, 2:281.
36. Margery Forester, *Michael Collins,* 213.
37. Dáil, *Debate on the Treaty,* 32.
38. Collins to Ackerman, 6/4/21, Collins Papers.
39. Collins to Clyde A. Beals, 26/8/21, *Ibid.*
40. Speech, Armagh, 4/9/21.
41. Interview with Talbot, 2/8/22.
42. Dáil, *Debate on the Treaty,* 36.
43. Interview with Talbot, 2/8/22.
44. T. M. Healy, *Letters and Leaders of My Day,* 644.
45. Dáil, *Private Sessions,* 262.
46. Interview with Talbot, 2/8/22.
47. Ó Muirthile 'Memoirs,' R. Mulcahy Papers, UCD.
48. Collins to O'Reilly, 11/11/21, Rex Taylor, *Michael Collins,* 121.

Chapter 3

1. Kathleen Napoli McKenna, 'In London with the Treaty Delegates: Personal Recollections,' *Capuchin Annual,* 1971, 322.
2. Collins to T. Maguire, P.P., 15/10/21, Collins Papers.
3. Ryan, *Remembering Sion,* 235.
4. Collins to J. O'Reilly, 11/10/21, Taylor, 121
5. Collins to de Valera, 12/10/21, Childers Papers, MS., 7790, TCD.
6. Collins, notes on British delegation, Taylor, 122.
7. *Ibid.*,124.
8. R. Murdoch, interview with R. Barton, *Sunday Press,* 19/9/71.
9. Collins, notes on British delegation, Taylor, 123-4.
10. Dorothy Macardle, *Irish Republic,* 530.
11. de Valera to Griffith, 14/10/21; except where otherwise noted all correspondence and documents relating to the London conference are in DE 2/304, SPO.
12. For a more in depth treatment of External Association, see author's forthcoming book, *De Valera's Foreign Policy.*
13. Seán Milroy, 'Memoirs,' Colum, 291.
14. Talbot, 145.
15. *Ibid.* 71-2; 149-50.
16. Collins to Kitty Kiernan, 16/10/21, Forester, 222.
17. Talbot, 151.
18. Report, Defence Committee meeting, 18/10/21.
19. Collins to Kiernan, 19/10/21,Forester, 222.

20. Collins to O'Kane, 19/10/21, Taylor, 124.
21. Calton Younger, *Ireland's Civil War,* 166.
22. Collins to O'Kane, 15/11/21, Taylor, 132.
23. Report, Third Plenary Session, 14/10/21.
24. *Ibid.*
25. Jones, 131.
26. Report, Third Plenary Session, 14/10/21.
27. Report, Fifth Plenary Session, 17/10/21.
28. Report Finance Committee meeting, 19/10/21.
29. Leon Ó Broin, 'Joseph Brennan,' *Studies,* Spring, 1977.
30. Collins to Childers, 29/10/21, Childers Papers, MS., 7794, TCD.
31. de Valera to Griffith, 19/10/21.
32. de Valera to Griffith, 22/10/21.
33. Childers to de Valera, 21/10/21.
34. Collins to O'Kane, n.d., Taylor, 136.
35. e.g. Childers to de Valera, 18/10/21; Childers to Brugha, 18/10/21.
36. Collins to O'Kane, 27/10/21, Taylor, 126.
37. Ulick O'Connor, *Oliver St. John Gogarthy,* 182-3; see reference to secret telegrams from Childers to de Valera in letter from N. S. Ó Nuallain to Marie O'Kelly (de Valera's secretary), 27/10/61, DE 2/304:2.
38. Jones, 3:141.
39. Pakenham, 148.
40. Griffith to de Valera, 24/10/21.
41. de Valera to Griffith, 25/10/21.
42. Delegation to de Valera, 26/10/21.
43. de Valera to Griffith, 27/10/21.
44. Griffith to Lloyd George, 2/11/21.
45. Griffith to de Valera,3/11/21.
46. de Valera to Griffith,9/11/21.
47. Collins to O'Kane, 2/11/21, Taylor, 130.
48. Collins to O'Kane, 4/11/21, Taylor, 132.
49. Collins to O'Kane, n.d. *Ibid.,* 136.
50. Collins to O'Kane, 17/11/21, *Ibid.,* 132.
51. Collins to nationalist delegation, n.d., Napoli Papers, MS., 22,773, NLI.
52. Collins to A.G., 24/10/21, Mulcahy Papers, P7A/72,UCD.
53. Cabinet minutes, 13/11/21, DE 2/238.
54. Barton to author, 1/10/69.
55. Chamberlain to Birkenhead, 25/11/21, Birkenhead, *F.E.,* 157.
56. Collins, memo., 23/11/21.
57. Dáil, *Private Sessions,* 194.
58. Griffith, memo., 28/11/21.
59. Griffith to de Valera, 29/11/21.
60. *Ibid.*

Chapter 4

1. de Valera to McGarrity, 27/12/21.
2. Childers, memo, 20/11/21.
3. Younger, 193.
4. Collins to O'Kane, 30/11/21, Taylor, 140.
5. Childers, Diary, 3/12/21, R.E. Childers Papers, MS 7819, TCD.
6. Stack, 'Own Account of Negotiation,' 16.
7. Ó Murchadha's notes of meeting of Cabinet and Delegation, 3/12/21.
8. Childers, Diary, 3/12/21.
9. Dáil, *Private Sessions,* 104.
10. Childers, Diary, 3/12/21.
11. de Valera to McGarrity, 27/12/21.
12. Ó Muirthile, 'Memoirs,' 170, Mulcahy Papers, P7A/209, UCD.
13. Dáil, *Private Sessions,* 104.
14. Stack, 16.
15. Dáil, *Private Sessions,* 177.
16. *Ibid.,* 118.
17. *Ibid.,* 115.
18. *Ibid.,* 186.
19. *Ibid.,* 187.
20. *Ibid.,* 189.
21. *Ibid.*
22. *Ibid.,* 191.
23. Childers, Diary, 3/12/21.
24. Dáil, *Private Sessions,* 187.
25. Taylor, 142-3.
26. Barton to author, 1/10/69.
27. Childers, Diary, 3/12/21.
28. Dáil, *Private Sessions,* 187.
29. Childers, Diary, 4/12/21.
30. Collins, Report of meeting with Lloyd George, 5/12/21.
31. Childers, Diary, 5/12/21.
32. Jones, *Whitehall Diary,* 3:180.
33. Collins, report of meeting, 5/12/21.
34. Barton, Report of two sub-conferences, 5-6/12/21.
35. Pakenham, 236.
36. Scott, *Political Diaries,* 412.
37. Chamberlain, *Down the Years.*
38. Churchill, *The Aftermath,* 306.
39. Barton's report.
40. Chamberlain, *Down the Years.*
41. Barton's actual notes taken during the meeting, Pakenham, 239.
42. *Freeman's Journal,* 6/12/21.
43. Griffith to de Valera, 6/12/21.
44. Childers, Diary, 5/12/21.
45. Lloyd George, *Is it Peace?*
46. Shakespeare, *Let Candles be Brought In,* 89.

47. Barton to Andrew Boyle, n.d., R.E. Childers Papers, MS. 7834,TCD.
48. Barton, interview with R. Murdoch, *Sunday Press,* 26/9/71 and 3/10/71.
49. Childers, Diary, 5/12/21.
50. *Ibid.,* 6/12/21.
51. Shakespeare, 90-1.
52. Shakespeare to author, 24/1/70.
53. Collins, *Path to Freedom,* 31.
54. *Ibid.,* 32.
55. Taylor, 141.
56. *Ibid.*
57. Birkenhead, *F.E.,* 163.
58. *Freeman's Journal,* 6/12/21.
59. Collins to O'Kane, 6/12/21.

Chapter 5

1. *Freeman's Journal,* 8/12/21.
2. Richard Mulcahy, Notes on Beaslaí's *Michael Collins,* MS., 168, Mulcahy Papers, P7/D1/67, UCD.
3. Stack, 18-9.
4. Stack, 19; Fitzgerald, review of *Peace by Ordeal, Observer,* 16/6/35.
5. Forester, 260.
6. Childers, Diary, 7/12/21, R.E. Childers Papers, MS. 7814, TCD.
7. Talbot, *Michael Collins' Own Story,* 153-4.
8. Stack, 19.
9. Collins, *Path to Freedom,* 30-1.
10. Barton, 'The Signing of the Treaty,' *Poblacht na h-Eireann,* 14/2/22.
11. Childers, Diary, 8/12/21.
12. Childers, notes of meeting, 8/12/21, Childers Papers, MS. 7819, TCD.
13. Childers, Diary, 8/12/21.
14. *Ibid.,* 8-9/12/21.
15. Stack, 19.
16. Batt O'Connor, *With Michael Collins in the Fight for Irish Freedom,* 180-2
17. Liam Lynch to Tom Lynch, Florence O'Donoghue, *No Other Law,* 190.
18. Ó Muirthile, 173.
19. Except where otherwise noted, the sources for the public and private debates in the Dáil are the respective official reports, *Debate on the Treaty,* and *Private Sessions of Second Dáil.*
20. Boyle and de Burca, *Free State or Republic?* 5.
21. de Valera to McGarrity, 27/12/21, McGarrity Papers.
22. Beaslaí 2:276.

23. Collins, *The Path to Freedom,* 43.
24. Healy, 2:645.
25. Collins to Kitty Kiernan, 20/12/21, Forester, 271.
26. Ryan, *Remembering Sion,* 278-9.
27. Forester, 271.

Chapter 6

1. Forester, 273.
2. Dáil, *Private Sessions,* 186.
3. *Freeman's Journal,* 24/12/21.
4. J. Anthony Gaughan, *Thomas Johnson,* 195.
5. *Freeman's Journal,* 4/1/22.
6. *Ibid.,* 5/1/22.
7. *Ibid.*
8. Michael Hayes, 'Dáil Éireann and the Irish Civil War,' 5-6.
9. *Freeman's Journal,* 7/1/22.
10. Beaslaí, 2:335.
11. Dáil, *Private Sessions,* 102.
12. *Irish Times,* 9/1/22.
13. Beaslaí, 2:338.
14. Collins to James K. McGuire, 18/1/22, Collins Papers.
15. Talbot, *Michael Collins' Own Story,* 159.
16. de Valera, *Speeches and Statements,* 98.
17. Speech in Waterford, 26/3/22.
18. de Valera to C. Ó Murchadha, 13/9/22.
19. Seanad, *Debates,* 20:1876.
20. de Valera, *Speeches and Statements,* 185.
21. de Valera, Proclamation, 16/4/22.
22. Boland to Austin Stack, 27/4/22, Stack Papers.
23. William O'Brien, *Forth the Banners Go,* 219-20.
24. de Valera, statement to press, 1/5/22.
25. Interview with John Steele of *Chicago Tribune, Poblacht na h-Éireann,* 18/5/22.
26. O'Kelly to Collins, 6/5/22, DE 2/514, SPO.
27. de Valera to Griffith, 16/10/21, DE 2/304, SPO.
28. Curran, *The Birth of the Irish Free State,* 204.
29. Collins to Seán T. O'Kelly, 15/6/22, DE 2/514, SPO.
30. L. Kohn, *The Constitution of the Irish Free State,* q. Harkness, 3.
31. de Valera to McGarrity, 10/9/22, McGarrity Papers.
32. Dwyer, *Eamon de Valera,* 79-98.
33. Collins, 'North East Ulster and the Treaty,' 28/2/22, Collins Papers.
34. Younger, 202.
35. Collins, notes, August 1922, Collins Papers.

Appendix

1. O'Hegarty, *A History of Ireland,* 754.
2. Mac Eoin to author, 20/3/70.
3. Blythe to author, 4/5/70.
4. *Ibid.*, 3/7/70.
5. *Ibid.*
6. Childers, Diary, 6/12/21; Dáil, *Private Sessions,* 135.
7. Stanley Salvidge, *Salvidge of Liverpool,* 224.
8. Birkenhead to Balfour, 3/3/22, *The Times,* 8/9/24.

Bibliography

This bibliography is intended only as a cross-reference to material mentioned in the text or notes. It does not purport to be a complete list of material consulted.

Manuscript Sources:

Childers, R. Erskine. Papers and Diaries, Trinity College, Dublin.

Collins, Michael, Papers, in possession of Liam Collins, Clonakilty, Co. Cork.

Dáil Éireann Files in DE 2 series, State Paper Office, Dublin.

Devoy, John. Papers, National Library of Ireland, Dublin.

Johnson, Thomas. Papers, National Library of Ireland, Dublin.

McGarrity, Joseph. Papers, National Library of Ireland, Dublin.

Mulcahy, Richard. Papers, University College, Dublin.

Napoli, Kathleen (nee McKenna). Papers, National Library of Ireland, Dublin.

O'Mara, James. Papers, Natioal Library of Ireland, Dublin.

Stack, Austin. Papers, in possission of Mrs Nanette Barrett (nee Stack), Tralee, Co. Kerry. This includes Stack's 'Own Account of Negotiations,' which has been extensively reproduced in Anthony Gaughan's *Austin Stack.*

Published Material:

Barry, Tom. *Guerrilla Days in Ireland;* Dublin, 1949.

Barton, Robert. 'Why Collins Signed,' interview with R. Murdoch, *Sunday Press,* 26 September 1971.

Beaslaí, Piaras. *Michael Collins and the Making of a New Ireland,* 2 vols., Dublin, 1926.

Birkenhead, Frederick, 2nd Earl of. *F.E.: The Life of F.E. Smith, First Earl of Birkenhead,* London, 1960.

Brennan, Robert, *Allegiance,* Dublin, 1950.

Chamberlain, Austen, *Down the Years,* London, 1935.

Churchill, Winston S. *The Aftermath,* London, 1929.

Collins, Michael. *The Path to Freedom,* Dublin, 1922, reprinted Cork, 1968.

Colum, Padraig. *Arthur Griffith,* Dublin, 1959.

Cronin, Seán. *The McGarrity Papers,* Tralee, 1972.

Crozier, Frank. *Ireland for Ever,* London, 1932.

Curran, Joseph M. *The Birth of the Irish Free State,* 1921-1923, Alabama, 1980.

Dáil Éireann. *Private Sessions of Second Dáil,* Dublin, n.d.

———— *Official Report: Debate on the Treaty between Great Britain and Ireland.* Dublin, 1922.

de Burca, Padraig and John F. Boyle. *Free State or Republic?* Dublin, 1922

de Valera, Eamon. *Speeches and Statements by Eamon de Valera,*

1917-1973, ed., M. Moynihan, Dublin, 1980.
Dwyer, T. Ryle. *Eamon de Valera,* Dublin, 1980.
——— *De Valera's Foreign Policy,* Dublin, 1982.
Figgis, Darrell. *Recollections of the Irish War,* London, 1927.
Forester, Margery. *Michael Collins: The Lost Leader,* London, 1971.
Gallagher, Frank. *The Anglo-Irish Treaty,* London, 1971.
Gaughan, J. Anthony. *Austin Stack,* Tralee, 1977.
——— *Thomas Johnson,* Dublin, 1980.
Hayes, Michael. 'Dáil Éireann and the Irish Civil War,' *Studies,* Spring, 1969.
Harkness, D.W., *The Restless Dominion,* London, 1969
Healy, T.M., *Letters and Leaders of My Day,* London, 1928.
Jones, Thomas. *Whitehall Diary, Vol. III: Ireland, 1918-25,* London, 1971.
Kee, Robert. *Ireland: A History,* London, 1981
Lloyd George, David. *Is it Peace?* London, 1923
Longford, Earl of, and Thomas P. O'Neill. *Eamon de Valera,* Dublin, 1970.
Macardle, Dorothy. *The Irish Republic,* London, 1968.
McCartan, Patrick. *With de Valera in America,* Dublin, 1932.
Macready, General Sir Neville. *Annals of an Active Life,* Vol. 2, London, 1924.
Nicholson, Harold. *King George V,* London, 1952.
O'Brien, William. *Forth the Banners Go,* Dublin, 1969.
O'Broin, Leon. 'Joseph Brennan, Civil Servant Extraordinary,' *Studies,* Spring, 1977.
——— *Michael Collins,* Dublin, 1980.
——— *Revolutionary Underground, The Story of the Irish Republican Brotherhood,* 1858-1924, Dublin, 1976.
O'Connor, Batt. *With Michael Collins in the Fight for Irish Independence,* London, 1929.
O'Connor, Frank. *The Big Fellow: Michael Collins and the Irish Revolution,* rev. ed., Dublin, 1965.
O'Connor, Ulick. *Oliver St John Gogarty,* London, 1964.
O'Donoghue, Florence. *No Other Law,* Dublin, 1954.
O'Hegarty, P.S., *A History of Ireland Under the Union, 1801-1922,* London, 1952.
O'Malley, Ernie. *Army Without Banners,* London, 1967.
Pakenham, Frank. *Peace by Ordeal,* rev. ed. London, 1967.
Riddell, Lord. *Intimate Diary of the Peace Conference and After, 1918-1923,* London, 1933.
Ryan, Desmond. *Remembering Sion,* London, 1934.
Salvidge, Stanley, *Salvidge of Liverpool,* London, 1934.
Shakespeare, Sir Geoffrey. *Let Candles Be Brought In,* London, 1949.
Talbot, Hayden. *Michael Collins' Own Story,* London, 1923.
Taylor, Rex. *Michael Collins,* London, 1958.
Winter, Ormonde. *Winter's Tale,* London, 1955.
Younger, Calton. *Ireland's Civil War,* London, 1968.

Index

MORE MERCIER BESTSELLERS

THE REAL CHIEF
The Story of Liam Lynch
Meda Ryan

Liam Lynch, Chief-of-Staff of the IRA, was known as 'The Chief' among Republicans, particularly in the First Southern Division.

Many of his comrades have wondered why he did not get the recognition which they felt he deserved, even though he had been offered the position as Commander-in-Chief of the Army in December 1921. Some felt that in the documentation of history De Valera overshadowed him while others thought that because of the firm stand he took in holding out for a Republic his deeds of bravery, especially before the Civil War, were down-graded.

But Liam Lynch is an extremely important figure in Irish history because of the part he played in gaining Irish Independence – first as Commandant of Cork No. 2 Brigade and later as Commandant of the First Southern Division. The part he played with Collins, Mulcahy and others in trying to avoid a Civil War and his efforts to achieve a Thirty-Two County Republic, rather than a partitioned State, should not be underestimated.

With the aid of Liam Lynch's personal letters, private documents and historical records, *The Real Chief* traces the turbulent career of one of Ireland's greatest guerrilla commanders. From his election in 1917 as First Lieutenant of the Irish Volunteer Company in Fermoy to the position of Chief-of-Staff of the Irish Republican Army, Lynch pledged, 'WE HAVE DECLARED FOR AN IRISH REPUBLIC AND WE WILL NOT LIVE UNDER ANY OTHER LAW.' He was determined, 'The war will go on until the independence of our country is recognised by our enemies, foreign and domestic.' This book also deals with the controversy which surrounds the death of *The Chief* when he was shot on the Knockmealdown Mountains on 10 April 1923.

SOUL OF FIRE
A Biography of Mary MacSwiney
Charlotte H. Fallon

Born during the Home Rule for Ireland Campaign, Mary MacSwiney was aware of the political situation in Ireland from an early age, though hers was not a politically involved home. Her awareness of Ireland's fight for self-government was sharpened during the Irish cultural revival of the early 1900s, her education and associations, and the political activities of her brother Terence.

At this time, however, Mary's energies were directed toward gaining voting rights for women, an issue she saw plainly as a matter of justice. With the rise of the Sinn Fein movement after 1912, her interest gradually shifted away from woman suffrage to nationalist concerns. With the Rising of 1916 and the declaration of the Republic, Mary came to believe that Ireland's desire for freedom, peace and prosperity could be best served by an Irish Republic totally outside the sceptre of British rule. From 1916 on, her life was devoted to the Republic and efforts at making it a functioning reality for all Irish men and women.

Her political career as a doctrinaire Republican brought her into conflict with the Catholic Church, the Free State Government against whom she waged two lengthy hunger strikes, those moderates within Ireland who believed in the 'stepping stone' approach to independence, and Eamon de Valera who she believed had forsaken the principles of 1916.

Her life provides information about women's issues in Ireland, Irish-American relations as she made two extensive fund raising tours of the United States, Irish Nationalism, the splintering of the Republican Movement, the rise of Irish Republican militancy, and the pervasive role of the Catholic Church in politics as well as in the rest of society.

MILESTONES IN IRISH HISTORY
Edited by Liam de Paor

Milestones in Irish History spans the whole range of time from early prehistory to the present, opening with Frank Mitchell's enquiry into the social and historical meaning of the building of the remarkable cemetery of megalithic tombs centred on the great monuments of Knowth, Dowth and Newgrange. Liam de Paor looks at the background and work of St. Patrick; Donnchadh Ó Corráin deals with Brian Boru and the Battle of Clontarf and Michael Richter examines the advent of the Normans.

Margaret MacCurtain discusses the Flight of the Earls and this is balanced, as it were, by an investigation of the new order that was created in its place in Aidan Clarke's look at the Plantations of Ulster. The Act of Union which made Ireland part of the United Kingdom in 1801 is examined by James McGuire and Kevin B. Nowlan looks at the career of Daniel O'Connell and Catholic Emancipation.

R.B. Walsh traces the decline of the Irish language and Donal McCartney examines the efforts to revive it at the turn of the century. Joseph Lee analyses the long drawn out struggle over the possession of land and Ronan Fanning gives his views on the partitioning of Ireland. John A. Murphy concludes with a look at the meaning of Ireland's entry to the EEC.

THE GREAT O'NEILL
Seán O'Faolain

The Great O'Neill first appeared in 1942 and the intervening years have only confirmed the book's standing as a modern classic and Seán O'Faolain's stature as one of the most distinguished of living Irish writers.

For nine years O'Neill resisted English expansion, became one of the most famous soldiers in Europe, wore out Elizabeth I, broke generals like Essex and Brough, involved Spain and Rome. Through these pages pass papal legates, government spies, great monarchs, statesmen, cutthroats, poisoners, passionate women, traitors and brave men. But, for all its drama, this book remains a work of scholarship and is likely to stand as the authoritative story of a crucial period of Irish history.

'May be commended to the historian for its breadth and freshness of view and the brilliance of its writing.'

The Times Literary Supplement

'A series of pictures of wild grandeur and outlandish brilliance set against a background of Renaissance colour and turmoil.'

Sunday Times

'A vivid fascinating picture of Elizabethan Ireland.'

Irish Times